**Getting There**

# Getting There

## Steps towards a green society

DEREK WALL

First published in 1990 by
Green Print
an imprint of The Merlin Press
10 Malden Road, London NW5 3HR



ISBN 1 85425 034 5

1 2 3 4 5 6 7 8 9 10 :: 99 98 97 96 95 94 93 92 91 90

Phototypeset by Input Typesetting, London

Printed in England by Biddles Ltd., Guildford, Surrey
on recycled paper

# DEDICATION

To all those who have been imprisoned or injured in the struggle for animal liberation.
And to Natasha Rzehorska.

# ACKNOWLEDGEMENTS

Numerous individuals have given me a push here or there, sparked off a new thought or helped by reading early drafts. In particular I would like to thank all of my 1988/89 second year Economics class at Bath College of Further Education, especially Kelvin Mottrem, Adrian Poole, Andrew Bolter, Matthew Hooper, Matthew Thomas and Karen Newman. Gavin Withers has put in an enormous amount of work into reading and correcting the text. Penny Kemp, Mary Mellor and Peter Tatchell have all made valuable comments as well as contributing directly. Tim Andrewes, Flo Bertelletti, Ian Coates, Harry Curtis, Steve Hunt, Malcolm and Linda Littledyke, Tim Morgan, John Norris, Barbara McPake, Dr David Pepper and Katharine Wall all read early drafts and supplied constructive feedback. Julia Leyden deserves thanks for introducing me to Green politics in the first place. Pete Campbell, Morag Deyes and Pete Taylor also deserve thanks. Members of the London Road Residents Association, in particular Ann and David Dunlop, Bath Animal Rights Group and Socialist Self-Management are all working in very different ways for a greener future and in their diversity give me inspiration. It excites me that people from so many very different backgrounds, political and social, are working towards similar goals. Finally, it has been a pleasure to work with an editor as sympathetic and patient as Jon Carpenter.

# Contents

# Foreword

The Green Party cannot afford to get it wrong. The Earth is in ecological crisis. The world is warming, and will continue to warm into the twenty-first century. John Gribbin, an authority on global warming, believes that the human race risks becoming extinct by the year 2200 unless change is urgently effected. The global crisis is real and will not go away without radical change to our lifestyles. Derek Wall opens the door to a credible alternative without compromise, arguing that decentralization, ecology, social justice and non-violence are principles that must be put into practice if we are to see our way out of the present worsening environment crisis.

However, the British Green Party has paid scant attention to detailed examination of its policies, and for much of the last sixteen years worthy principles sufficed. Now, with 15% of the vote in the 1989 European elections, it is more urgent than ever to conduct that examination. The debate on green economics has hardly started. Much has been written on the need for an alternative economic system but the actual process of 'how to get there' has been sadly neglected. In this book, Derek Wall starts the process. He has been researching into green economics for many years now. His invaluable work for the Association of Socialist Greens and the British Green Party means that he, more than most, knows the necessity for a comprehensive review of green economics.

It is the question of economic growth that has been central to the green critique of modern industrial countries. It is where greens part company with mainstream politicians. The recent conversion of the leaders of the established political parties to the 'green' cause falls short of any true acceptance of the 'limits of growth'. In fact both the Conservative and Labour parties advocate continuing industrial economic expansion as necessary to generate the finances to pay for cleaning up environmental degradation. The Social and Liberal Democratic Party talk of sustainable growth but make no attempt to challenge the capitalist economy. The Labour Party Policy Review is designed purely for electoral success and falls short of any examination of the ecological crisis, despite its green rhetoric. Derek Wall recognizes that capitalism is incompatible with ecology but he also acknowledges that traditional state socialism will not work either.

In the late 1970s and early 1980s, the more radical Labour local authorities, such as the Greater London Council and Sheffield, devoted more time to developing local economic strategies and environmental programmes, but were halted by central government in any attempt to implement their programmes. The new left are beginning to examine the green critique but I have a sneaking suspicion that it is more to do with their marginality under the present Labour leadership than with a wholesale conversion to green politics. The Socialist Conference, now in its fourth year, still leaves green issues on the fringe of the debate despite protestations from green socialists to make them central. There seems to be a fear of discussing such issues as the question of production for 'need' not 'greed' for fear of upsetting the trade union movement. Until consultation and debate within the trade union movement is under way, the arguments on limits to growth will sadly be left with the more forward looking greens, socialists and individual trade union members. Yet such issues as health and safety at work, transport, and toxic waste disposal are as central to the trade union movement as they are to the green movement. Until progress is made with discussions with the unions, it will be difficult to get workforces to accept the urgency of the ecological crisis and the necessity of accepting different ways of working and changing patterns of industrial output.

The Green Party must not fall into the trap of becoming a conventional political party. Its strength lies in that it offers a radical alternative based on empowering people to take the critical decisions that affect their lives. It must not lose its reputation for honesty and truthfulness. It must not fall into the leadership trap that the media so desperately wants it to. Leaders can be knocked down, and with them the movement they are trying to create. Green politics is too important and urgent for any kind of hiccup. Nor must it give in to those vested interests that will be trying so hard for compromise. It will be difficult, but by resisting those inevitable pressures to compromise, it will win out in the long run. The Green Party must not forget that it is opening new ground and challenging previously entrenched beliefs. Until peoples' hearts and minds have changed, it is questionable whether electoral politics can be seen as the only path to follow.

The more the ecological crisis is recognised, the more international co-operation will become. Greens, by their very nature, are an international non-violent movement and in future decades will play an increasingly significant role. Already green movements exist in East and West, in developed and less developed countries. The richer industrial countries have enormous responsibility to help the less developed countries in their struggle for a more equitable distribution of the world's resources. At present, 80 per cent of the world's resources are consumed by just 20 per cent of the world's population. This is just not sustainable and Greens must be vociferous in their condemnation of the present system. The myth perpetuated for decades that capitalism will alleviate poverty can now be seen for what it is – an illusion. Capitalism needs poverty in order to survive. The gains of some are always at the expense of others and at the very bottom of the pile are the countries of the Third World. Solidarity is needed between Greens in all corners of the globe. As an international movement, we can do much to bring to the attention of the world's people the glaring inequalities between rich and poor and the connections between industrialization and the ecological crisis. For example, the mounting indebtedness of the less developed countries could bring about global ecocide unless green solidarity prevails. Greens in Europe have done much to contribute to the debate on debt crisis and slowly world leaders are listening to their arguments. But we have a long way to go and it is very urgent. As we increase demands for more of the world's natural resources, nature is quietly and firmly paying us back. We may not be able to afford her interest. We are an integral part of nature, not her masters or mistresses. We must get the message across.

In challenging our very belief systems, Derek Wall gives us

a new way of looking at and developing political theory. He guides us chapter by chapter on a journey through green politics: the end result is a thoughtful and well researched book providing both questions and answers. While Derek would not argue that his book is the green 'bible', it nevertheless moves the debate considerably forward. As he puts it, 'Green politics is possible, green economics will be very much more difficult.' We have much to thank him for. A Green revolution is possible.

Penny Kemp
October 1989

# Introduction

Given the unsustainable nature of modern Western society and the ecological crisis that threaten all of us, the need for a different kind of society is obvious: much has been written on the subject. The *type* of society we must move towards and *how* we get there is a subject which has been discussed far less.

In one sense, the Green movement, for all its criticisms of ecological destruction, economic injustice, an accelerating arms race and late twentieth-century commodity fetishism, is profoundly apolitical. If politics is the art of the possible the Greens remain little more than an ineffectual pressure group.

The debate on how to get to a Green society has hardly started. Greens, from Edward Goldsmith (editor of the influential magazine *The Ecologist* that helped launch Friends of the Earth and the then Ecology Party) to Jonathon Porritt in the eighties, have tended to see the task principally in terms of electing a Green government and passing laws. Indeed, the whole point of *Blueprint for Survival*[1], a report produced by Goldsmith and supported by many prominent scientists, was to persuade governments to move towards an economy based on ecological sustainability instead of expansion and, failing this, to launch a new 'Movement for Survival'. Such a 'Green' party would win seats and put Ecotopia on the statute books. Ever since, Green politics has almost exclusively meant electoral politics; yet despite fast worldwide growth such an approach is not without its problems. Progress, for example, has been blocked by a lack of proportional representation in English-speaking countries like Canada, the U.S.A. and Britain. Recent developments in Moscow[2] suggest that Greens will be elected in the U.S.S.R. before they reach Westminster or Washington. 'Ecology in one country', given the lack of respect pollution has for international boundaries, is an even more unworkable concept than that of socialism. Certainly countries as influential as the U.S.A. must be greened as a priority.

How positive change is to be achieved, given the millions of dollars spent by presidential candidates and the Democrat/Republican stranglehold, is a question which merits infinitely more discussion than it has so far received.

Even where Greens have been more successful as in West Germany, the system works so as to either exclude or dilute their radical demands. Either Greens stand by their principles, losing direct influence and being accused as in Hamburg of supporting Conservative politicians through default, or they enter into reformist alliances with Social Democrats eager to 'gobble them up like spinach.'

Systems tend to perpetuate themselves. To ensure our ultimate biological survival, Green politics will have to turn our present systems upside down. The deficiencies of the political system are obvious; the contradictions of our economic system are even more startling and will be far more difficult to correct. Simply put, our economic system demands continual economic growth: we must consume more, waste more and use more; we must produce more children, eat more Big Macs and watch more television. Otherwise profits, reinvestment capital, jobs, government spending, indeed the whole world economy, will be under threat. By its very nature the capitalist system has to keep growing for ever, but it is difficult to see how much growth can be sustained at all, let alone sustained without doing long term damage to our planet and future generations.[3]

How to introduce a new and workable alternative to capitalism is a question which has eluded three centuries of socialist thinkers; it is a question the Greens must answer clearly and quickly for the most material reason of all. Design, of everything from landscapes to fridges, from toasters to town plans, will have to become Green. The technical problems of building goods to last, of promoting local production for local need, of making items less energy- and resource-hungry, will all demand very careful deliberation. Scientific research into the ecological damage done to our planet and its capacity to coexist with humankind will be vital. Such research will of necessity be holistic, linking population densities, biological cycles and marine eco-systems; in fact so complex as to appear almost impossible. The economic problem of providing incentives to encourage the production of longer-lasting goods will be difficult to overcome, and even when it is, the challenge of making such technology decentralized and humane will not be met easily.

Perhaps the most difficult and controversial task of all will be to challenge entrenched views and tackle a belief system (or as Gramsci put it, a 'hegemony')[4] which has evolved to support the demands of consumerism. What will Greens do about *The Sun*, let alone the multi-media empire its proprietor is building? How will the Greens resist the inevitable pressure from the vested interests they challenge, whether media smears or armed state repression? The City and multinationals will hardly allow their profits to be taken away in the name of sustainability without putting up a fight and it is these institutions that give the modern state most of its power. Large corporations have more power than medium sized countries and they won't hesitate to use it whether in the form of economic sabotage, disinformation or old fashioned military force, if they feel that their interests are being challenged. The question of how we will non-violently win the 'battle for the planet' has never been addressed by the Porritts and Goldsmiths of the Green movement.

For good or for ill, the Green movement lacks its own Machiavellis, Lenins, and Gandhis. Greens need Green political theory; they need to be clear about both ends and means; they need to think through how we are to get to a Green society. There are no simple solutions to complex problems; different individuals will need, in different contexts, to pursue diverse strategies. While radicalism literally means going to the roots of a problem, it is dangerously reductionist to tackle just one root; the failure of the traditional left has been due mainly to economic reductionism. There will never be a definitive handbook of ecologically sound political theory; the task of this volume is to provoke debate but if it does not provoke action it will have failed. What is needed is committed, coherent action on the part of people in every area of the globe. As Schumacher was fond of saying an ounce of practice is worth a ton of theory. The point, to paraphrase Marx, is not merely to describe the world but to change it. And change it we must, if we, our children and our planet are to have a future.

# 1
# Another green world?

## In defence of partial Utopia

Although others have given varied and detailed descriptions of a future Green society, I feel it is necessary to describe my personal concept. Both because it varies in some respects from earlier models and because I believe that it is important to work out at least roughly where one is going before discussing how to get there. Marxists have criticized such an approach arguing that 'utopias' or plans of possible future societies are more 'compensatory than emancipatory', and distract from the real task of changing society.[1] Alternative visions become a way of compensating for political impotency instead of seeking to overcome it. Green utopias have also been attacked as being oppressive. *Blueprint for Survival* was more or less a plan for forced decentralization and the division of Britain into communes by a benevolent but strongly centralized one party Westminster government. In Callenbach's novel, 'Ecotopia' is protected by threatening to blow up New York with hidden nuclear explosives in the event of interference from outsiders![2] But even if such ecofascist excesses are rejected, one person's 'utopia' will almost inevitably be someone else's dystopia (anti-utopia) if translated too literally into reality.

Even so it is vital to have some vision of the future. Marx, by rejecting utopias and failing to discuss in even the barest detail his conception of a communist society, left the door open for the excesses of Stalin and Mao. If there is no initial vision one will be supplied later on; it is far better to have different models open to critical attention from day one than to have to choose at the last minute, when the prevailing order is collapsing and looks likely to be replaced with something even worse. Utopias can emancipate if they inspire us to work towards a vision of something better. As Oscar Wilde noted, 'A map of the world that does not include Utopia is not even worth glancing at, for it leaves out the one country at which Humanity is always landing . . . Progress is the realization of Utopias.'[3]

Nobody can or should try to give an exactly detailed description of a future society. Blueprints won't work. Societies grow through historical processes and a Green world will (hopefully) grow through mass participation. Despite the efforts of William Morris and Aldous Huxley, amongst others, the future won't come in the form of a novel. But even if we consign these utopias to literature, we will still need a guide as to where we are going before setting off on the journey. This author's approach is to argue that a Green society will have to function within a variety of constraints or parameters and that it is more important to define these however crudely than to draw a brick by brick architects plan of definitive The Green Society. A variety of different potential Green societies exist, the question explored throughout this book being, how can people be empowered to make a choice? The rest of this chapter tries to define the boundaries and briefly reviews where we are crossing them at present. In my view a Green world would have to be ecologically sustainable (the most important constraint), economically viable and socially just. Sustainability, viability and justice have and will remain areas of intense debate.

## Ecological sustainability

Dealing with the first set of constraints it is possible to say with conviction that if we destroy the global environment or destabilize it enough, we will destroy ourselves, and that a society that transgresses ecological boundaries will find itself in trouble. Any political philosophy that forgets biological restraints is bankrupt and can be swiftly rejected as a complete solution to our problems; ecological constraints are fundamental. Defining them with any confidence is more problematic. 'Ecosystems tend towards stability . . . the more diverse and complex the ecosystem the more stable it is; that is, the more species and the more they inter-relate, the more stable is their environment,' argued *Blueprint for Survival*.[4] Stability may further be defined as the ability of a system to withstand external change – in this case the global life-support system. Such stability is under threat in hundreds of ways. Environmentalists have compared the extinction of any one plant or animal to the removal of a rivet from an aircraft in flight. We don't know how many pins can be removed without the wings falling off, yet despite the dangers we continue taking them out! At least 25,000 species are under threat and as one researcher notes, 'The more new data added, the worse the picture looks . . .'[4] Western Ecuador alone is said to have lost up to 50,000 separate species in the last 25 years.[5] The rivets are dropping out of the sky with the destruction of wetlands, forests and increased development leading to the loss of other varied habitats.

Monocultures devoid of species other than those directly productive to humans (particularly humans in the pursuit of profit!) are encouraged, despite the dangers of such uniformity. Central and South American governments give tax incentives to companies that cut down tropical forests, replacing the richest habitats with the greatest diversity with stage one of the burger chain.[6] The European Community has actually banned many traditional crops. Since 1970 multinationals have bought up 839 seed companies, and as a result North American stockists have dropped 263 varieties of open-pollenated vegetables; 'Their reasons include low profitability, the possibility of farmers producing their own seeds, and lower dependence of older varieties on corporate-made pesticides and fertilizers.'[7] Species are retained on the basis of appearance and shelf life: taste and nutrition are of secondary importance. Restricting or abolishing species that do not need pesticides or fertilizers is an excellent way of increasing the profits of large chemical companies and oil producers who have bought up many of the seed banks. The situation is apparently even worse for fruit trees and those producing nuts that could provide low cost protein which might help the 'First World' to be less dependent on the 'Third World'. Zoos and seed museums cannot replace living habitats nor account for all of the vast natural genetic variation within a species. Remedial action has been slow. Industrial development is apparently more important than the preservation of an obscure type of emerald ant or unusual shrubs. 'Advocates of perpetual economic growth treat living species as expendable. As a result, an extreme crisis of unprecedented magnitude is under way. Worse yet, when diversity needs help most, it is neglected and misunderstood by much of the scientific community that once championed it.'[8]

The oceans, which support the biological cycles basic to life (carbon, nitrogen, sulphur and phosphorus) are in trouble. A cocktail of pollution, including PCBs, dioxins, low- and high-level nuclear waste and heavy metals, pour into our seas. The INF treaty has shifted the missiles off the land and into the holds of nuclear submarines (several of which have been lost on the ocean floor). The problems of the North Sea are well publicized but not exceptional. To take just one trivial example, 6.4 million tons of shipboard litter are dumped every year killing 1 million sea birds and over 100,000 seals, dolphins and whales.[9] Even the oceans are too small to absorb unlimited human pollution caused by unlimited human expectations.

Inter-tidal zones along coast lines and continental shelves maintain the oceans and seas. Where '. . . dissolved organic and inorganic nutrients and detrital material enter the marsh estuary from inflowing rivers and streams, they are met by a wedge of salt water pushed along the bottom by the incoming tide. The mixing of these nutrient-rich waters is the basis for a diverse food chain capable of supporting a host of near shore marine life, including the larval and juvenile stages of commercially important fish and shellfish.'[10]

Yet ever since Roman attempts to drain the Pontine Marshes, salty fens, swamps, estuaries and mud flats have been seen as sources of disease that need draining and sterilizing. Puerto Rico has now lost a quarter of its mangrove swamp, Thailand has lost 20% of its original inter-tidal habitats.[11] To make matters worse flooding caused by the greenhouse effect will shift sea levels across the world and cause further disruption. But even escaping such drastic change, the inter-tidals will continue to be eroded by industry, agriculture and tourism in every part of the globe.

The tropical forest will be gone within fifty years.[12] Japan illegally imported 1 million cubic metres of timber from the Philippines in 1986.[13] Despite recent land reform and protection moves, traditional farmers are still being attacked by armed loggers and tree cover has fallen from 75% of the islands' surfaces to a mere quarter. As the forests burn or are felled they release methane and carbon dioxide increasing the greenhouse effect and drastically reducing species and systems diversity. Already deforestation is having a 'significant effect on atmospheric chemistry.'[14] Much of the destruction has been funded by the World Bank.[15] New roads open up new areas of forest to the chainsaw, the axe and the match and we foot the bill for such investment aid. Our hunger for resources fuels the damage. In 1967, eighteen billion tons of high grade ore – copper, manganese, nickel, cassiterite and bauxite – were discovered in the Carajas mountains of Brazil. $14.5 billion funding on the part of development banks, private investors and the Brazilian government has helped open up the area. 15,000 square miles of forest will be cut down. Glossy brochures from the Banco Itau aimed at U.S. investors cite Brazil's 'less stringent anti-pollution legislation' as just one attraction.[16]

The deserts expand as the forests contract. An area of 60,000 square miles across an astonishing ninety-four countries, disappears into the arid wastes every year. In the Sudan, the sands have come 100 kilometres in a decade. In Ethiopia the situation will soon be as bleak. Even dry grasslands help feed 850 million people and produce valuable plants like the jojoba bush adding diversity to the global jigsaw; in short they are of much greater value both economically and ecologically than dunes.[17] Much of the aid to desert zones has, as with the rainforests, been spent on roads that bring more people in and increase population pressures, rather than on intelligent conservation measures. Over-exploitation is made worse by cash crops that push the hungry on to the most marginal land. While millions died in the Sahel, thousands of tons of 'foodstuffs' were exported to Europe and North America. The deserts advance, the peasants die, we drink our coffee.[18]

The temperate forests of the northern hemisphere have almost all gone (at least in relation to original virgin wildwood), destroyed by Greek goats and Roman ploughs.[19] Their absence makes us poorer and the role of the existing tropical forests even more important in regulating biological processes. The Mesolithic hunter-gatherers of post-Ice Age Britain inhabited a colder version of a Brazilian forest, full of fungi, small game, edible plants and other easily caught or picked delicacies.[20] By the Bronze Age most of Britain's wilderness had gone. Our national parks of Dartmoor, the Lake District, Yorkshire and the Scottish moors disguise peaty, human-made disaster areas, all originally afforested, all cut down by our ancestors. To an extent new forests have made up for the loss but only in a limited way. Nothing planted by us can match what evolved from nature. Acid rain is destroying the Black Forest and the huge belts of woodland across Central and Eastern Europe. According to Friends of the Earth a quarter of British trees are dying from acid damage.[21]

The ice caps and immediate environs, despite the thinning of the ozone layer, the opening up of Siberia and the possible post-Falklands War exploitation of the Antarctic, seem relatively safe by comparison. But the greenhouse effect threatens them with rising seas and higher temperatures. Not even penguins will be safe from the effect of coal fires and charred rainforests. As the tundra melts, huge quantities of liquid peat will decay and release methane – a potent greenhouse gas – that will feed back into higher temperatures and even greater damage.

Soils are being eroded, not only in the areas of encroaching desert, but across the globe from East Anglia, where dust storms have been known to block roads, to the mid-west of the U.S.A., where the recent droughts have frightened farmers. Monocultures of crops in neat rows, with bare ground in between, invite erosion. As fields grow and hedges disappear the problem is made worse. As marginal land (particularly on hill slopes) is cultivated, soil is blown or washed away. It has to go somewhere: already islands have formed in the Indian Ocean as Nepalese fields are reincarnated in mudflats in the Bay of Bengal.

There is now a consensus that weather patterns will change dramatically. Already after just two centuries of industrial growth, the Earth's temperature is rising faster than perhaps at any other time in its history. Emissions of carbon dioxide ($CO_2$) from the burning of coal, oil and natural gas cause the notorious greenhouse effect. No one knows exactly what will happen but as temperatures increase, the oceans will expand, ice caps melt and sea levels rise. As eco-systems suffer yet another shock, extinctions will increase and biological stability will be reduced.

James Lovelock has argued with the aid of his Gaia hypothesis that the whole planet is one self-regulating life support system (Gaia being the Greek Earth goddess) and that fossil fuels were laid down millions of years ago to reduce the quantity of $CO_2$ in the atmosphere and maintain a temperature equilibrium suitable for life – an equilibrium that human progress is now inevitably destroying by burning such fossil fuels and releasing the trapped gases as fast as it can.[22] The rich countries of the North will be able to build massive defences against the rising water – poorer countries like the Maldives and Bangladesh will just disappear. The number of environmental refugees will be massive; the racism with which they will be met, by the citizens of the countries who caused them to be refugees, will no doubt be greater still.

Carbon dioxide is only part of the problem. Other greenhouse gases include methane (given off by decaying rubbish, animal dung and paddy fields), nitrous oxides (produced by fertilizers) and chlorofluorocarbons (from aerosols, freezer cooling units and packaging). Not only does each molecule of CFC trap 10,000 times more heat than one of $CO_2$, they destroy the ozone layer which protects us from the sun's deadly ultra-violet rays.[23] Since 1970 chlorine concentrations in the atmosphere have risen from 1.5 parts per billion (ppb) to 3ppb and are predicted to top 5ppb by the year 2000. As one authority has put it, 'To get back to 1.5ppb we will have to cut production of CFC's by 95 per cent. Even then we would be stuck with the ozone hole over the Antarctic for at least 50 years.'[24] 655,000 tons of CFCs are released through the use of aerosols, refrigeration units and packaging every year. The US Environment Protection Agency estimates that while there has been a 30% reduction of the ozone layer above the Antarctic, a mere 5% drop over more populated areas could lead to an extra 15,000 cases of skin cancer.[25] Crops, already affected by acid rain, will be damaged. Ocean-dwelling plankton that absorb carbon dioxide will be killed by ultraviolet rays and thus reinforce the greenhouse effect.

While we destroy the skies, authorities like Rosalie Bertell argue that nuclear radiation is warping and eroding the very structure of our most intimate tissues, wrecking our genetic material and passing the damage on from generation to generation.[26] A host of dangerous chemicals compound the threats to eco-systems, key biochemical cycles and DNA. Every year 1,000 new chemicals join the 70,000 odd compounds (many of which are dangerous) in daily use. 'O.E.C.D countries were able to recycle, reclaim, or reuse only 12–16 million metric tons of hazardous wastes, roughly 4–5 per cent of the total amount generated in 1984.'[27] Lead, DDT and nuclear fallout litter the fatty tissues of every human being, penguin and porcupine on this planet. The long list of dangers reads like something out of an undergraduate ecology textbook and could be continued almost indefinitely. There are other cycles, other eco-systems and other pollutants we know little or nothing of. Most worrying of all the scientists don't know either.

Ecological parameters are difficult to calculate. They may even be beyond what human beings – just one species amongst many – are capable of understanding. 'Nature is bountiful, but it is also fragile and finely balanced. There are thresholds that cannot be crossed without endangering the basic integrity of the system. Today we are close to many of these . . .', warned the Brundtland report.[28]

For all we know, we may have pushed the planet's life-support system into a dangerous state of positive feedback, whereby change induces a reinforced chain reaction of destruction. It may already be too late to take remedial action. We can only hope that the situation hasn't gone too far and look for ways of healing the destruction we have already wrought.

Although we don't yet fully understand the consequences of our action, the dangers are obvious. We cannot afford to wait any longer before taking action. '. . . With ruined habitats and impoverished and malfunctioning ecosystems within a short distance of every reader of this article – it is wrong to waste time by indulging the apologists of the status quo with scientific games and numerical nit-picking,' argued Ehrenfeld writing in *New Scientist.*[29]

There are obvious lessons for any future society. If we use ever increasing quantities of energy, the Earth will become either thermally or radioactively too hot to handle. It may take some time but it will happen and we are unlikely to find the wait a pleasant one. If we consume more and more, we will destroy the oceans and tropical forests which maintain life. We have to cut consumption, reject economic growth and protect species and eco-systems. The 1988 Toronto conference asked for a gradual 20% cut in fossil fuel consumption to combat the threat of $CO_2$ emissions. This almost certainly errs on the side of political rather than biological pragmatism. Continued use of coal, oil, gas, peat and other fossil fuels has already led to the production of more $CO_2$ than biological systems can mop up.

Coal burning can be cleaned up using the fluidized bed and other methods to scrub out sulphurs and nitrates that form acid rain, but it still has its ecological dangers. Neither strip mining nor oil refining are environmentally benign. $CO_2$ cannot be removed. Even if it could, where would it be stored? Some have suggested recycling it into soft drinks!

> To feed each American, about 1500 litres of oil equivalents are expended per year. Furthermore, a total of 17 per cent of United States energy is expended to supply the population with food. Of this, agricultural production uses about 6 per cent, food processing and packaging use another 6 per cent, while distribution and home preparation account for the remaining 5 per cent.[30]

Given statistics like these and the assumption that energy use is likely to increase amongst developing countries, the 'First World' will have to cut back drastically. Non-energy resource use will have to be cut as well. A whole host of toxins will have to be banned outright. Disruption of the nitrogen cycle demands that we use less inorganic fertilizer. Ecological realities demand that we live better on less.

## Economic viability

Even if ecological factors are defined and accepted, economic realities will have to be addressed. Often ecological and economic restraints are closely linked; as many Greens have pointed out the environment is the base of all economic activity and if we destroy it we destroy ourselves at the same time. Conversely if we solve our ecological problems at the cost of destroying the economy we will remain in trouble. As it is, global economic cycles are just as much under threat as their ecological equivalents.

Increasingly, economic activity is created through the need to solve the problems of pollution, resource depletion and human alienation caused by earlier economic growth. As Greens have pointed out for decades, our yardsticks of prosperity and growth more often than not measure negative factors such as increased weapons expenditure and the cost of cleaning oil spillages. Non-monetary economic activity such as allotment production or voluntary work goes unrecorded. The global economic crisis is about more than poor or perverse indicators. We live in an astonishingly unfair world. While the USA with five per cent of the world's population uses 22 per cent of the world's resources, the developed world as a whole with a third of the world's population uses 90% of all resources. In the 'Third World' only a small minority have any real share of the small quantity of wealth that such countries manage to hold on to. 'In El Salvador in 1979, two per cent of the total population owned sixty per cent of arable land.' One per cent of Haitians hold approximately 44% of national income, 80% of the population survive on about $100 a year, the lucky ones work for US companies assembling baseballs and electronic clothing for about 33 cents an hour on average. Americans put more fertilizer on their lawns and tennis courts than India uses for all purposes. In the Caribbean where 80 per cent of children are malnourished, nearly half the land is used to grow cash crops to enrich a small local elite.[31] Our greed directly creates their need. The 'Third World' is a product of colonialism and neo-colonialism. Growth, rather than feeding people, starves them by producing cattle feed instead of human staples, export crops instead of food for starving children, plus the high prestige projects; cathedrals in the Ivory Coast, Brazillian cities in the desert, motorways to nowhere. Arms to keep the peasants from rising up and taking back their land are another element of GNP. As Ryszard Kapuscinski argued while discussing the causes of the Ethiopian famine,

> Usually it is said that periodic droughts cause bad crops and therefore starvation. But it is the elites of starving countries that propagate this idea. It is a false idea. The unjust or mistaken allocation of funds and national property is the most frequent source of hunger. There was a lot of grain in Ethiopia, but it had first been hidden by the rich and then thrown on the market at a doubled price, inaccessible to peasants and the poor. Figures about the hundreds of thousands who starved next to abundantly stocked granaries were published. On the orders of local dignitaries, the police finished off whole clans of still-living human skeletons.[32]

As Trainer puts it, 'A market economy is an ingenious device for ensuring that when things become scarce only the rich can get them.'[33] We live in a global economy which is incredibly wasteful, with billions of pounds spent on trinkets and televisions, burnt overheating office buildings, used to feed domestic pets instead of people and gambled away in thousands of trivial ways. All of this is at the cost of our environment, the 'Third World' and future generations in our society who will have no access to the resources we have squandered. Our economy relies on institutionalized cruelty to other species with millions of chickens, cattle and pigs forced into factory farming and vivisection (to test more shampoos, cosmetics and often unnecessary or brand name versions of existing drugs) that causes more suffering than ever before in human history. Animal abuse is at the heart of the holocaust we call our economy.

The economy is wildly unstable as well as unjust. In minutes billions can be wiped off the face value of shares and within 90 seconds a stock market crash is transmitted around the world with disastrous results. Government policy is no longer independent. Foreign multinationals have enormous power not least over employment and can effectively flit from country to country. A strong exchange rate can only be maintained with injections of short term finance or 'hot money' that rushes around the globe at an ever accelerating rate. Capital flights triggered by policies with which the money markets disagree can quickly bring any economy to it fiscal knees.

World banking is in trouble. While the standard practice of only backing up loans with a small quantity of notes and coins sounds precarious, it hasn't stopped bankers from providing investment and making secure profits. During the 1980s, though, things have become more difficult. In the early 1970s oil money was lent by major banks to developing countries at a time when interest rates were very low. (Much of the ecological destruction reviewed above was funded in this way.) Recession and higher interest rates have multiplied debt world-wide from \$60 billion in 1973 to a massive \$900 billion in 1984.[34] By 1982 some countries needed more than their total export earnings merely to pay back debt repayments and interest.[35] The debt crisis has prompted cutbacks in the poorest parts of the world. It also threatens world wide finance. In 1984, the 12th largest US bank, the Continental Illinois, had to be rescued at a cost of $4.5 billion to the US taxpayer. Even if only a minority of depositors attempted to remove their money, the resulting 'run on the bank' could unravel the whole system. Put another way, 'Major defaults would threaten the stability of major world banks and perhaps the whole capitalist financial system.'[36]

There are other more obvious but no less serious problems. Despite low inflation and unemployment in the 1950s and 1960s, in the 80s the effect of tackling one appears to be a sharp rise in the other. Keynesianism is dead and monetarism has failed. Economics isn't working. The creation of a single European market, the recent free-trade agreements between the US and Canada and economic reforms in the Soviet Union will all tend to make the world economically more uniform. Economic monocultures are as dangerous as ecological ones.

As we have already noted economic and ecological problems are closely linked but more often than not the solution to one set of problems is a cause of the other. Politicians demand that we grow our way out of crisis, yet as we have seen such growth is impossible without straining to breaking point the cycles that maintain life. Conservatives demand that firms become more competitive and that industry is freed from both red and green tape. The British Labour Party sees nothing inconsistent between calls for 5 per cent annual growth in G.N.P. and their new found Green concerns. While environmental constraints mean abandoning affluence, conserving energy and resources and putting economic growth into reverse, zero economic growth, let alone negative, will turn our present economic system upside down. Nearly all of us expect higher standards of living. Capitalism cannot function without economic growth. Governments demand that we work harder, producing more and consuming more so as to reduce unemployment and get the economy going. Firms must grow, if they are to overtake the growth of rivals in the constant race to make larger profits that can be re-invested in ever more sophisticated capital equipment and promote further growth.

Decoupling prosperity from growth sounds like madness from the point of view of conventional economics but the alternative is biological collapse. A starting point is economic justice – if the cake ceases to grow it will have to be cut up more fairly. There will be a need to redistribute from rich to poor both within the north of the globe and from North to South. The idea that a small, elite minority will live in pampered conditions while the rest steal from each other, scraping their pennies and roubles together to pay poll tax or IMF debt repayments, continuing to wreck the earth in the search for a daily crust, is unacceptable. It is both wicked and impractical to punish the poor for the crimes of an economic system set up to serve the rich.

Economic democracy is just as important. Ordinary people need more say in economic decisions. Economic power is becoming ever more centralized as Westminster takes control of local authorities and Strasbourg tries to take control of Westminster. In reality multinational companies are growing in influence and all other forces are declining. Local economic planning, along with local investment banks geared to financing what is important to communities, will become increasingly pragmatic in a world where the roulette wheels of the international stock market cease to be a stable means of deciding our future. Need should replace greed (i.e. effective demand backed up by cash) as the priority for allocating resources at a decentralized level. There should be more equal access to the means of production and sustenance. At present cats have more purchasing power and influence than the poor of this planet. Accidents of geography and colonial history should no longer determine who gets the fish.

A basic income scheme whereby everyone is guaranteed a minimum amount to live on, together with a concerted attempt to house the homeless (perhaps through self-build and co-op schemes), will be vital. 'If hardship is even a possibility, a sense of insecurity will prevent individuals from acting in accordance with ecological constraints. A guarantee of security will not ensure voluntary ecological behaviour, but it is a necessary precondition.'[37] Economic activity needs to become more diverse and less dependent on abstract market forces. A single world economy is less stable than a multi-faceted one based on the activities of billions of people at a local level. Ultimately Greens will need to go back to the traditional basis of economics: the study of how scarce resources can be used to meet real human needs. Conventional economic practice which consumes scarce resources at ever increasing rates while constantly creating new 'needs', is even on its own terms ridiculous and unsustainable. A Green society would have to meet needs on a deep level.

It may be scarcity rather than surplus that will liberate us. Having less, if goods are made to last longer and shared, will mean more. Increased leisure, if used for creativity and self-realization instead of as a way of consuming, will increase our real standard of living.

## Social justice

Finally, a Green society will have to work within social constraints. A Green future will fail if it leaves the vast majority of the population dissatisfied. Even passive tolerance won't be enough for it to function; a Green society will demand strong communities, communities unlikely to exist if social frustration leads even a large minority to isolated individual hedonism, serious crime, addiction to hard drugs like heroin or desperate over-consumption of soft ones from alcohol to TV soap operas. At present we live in a society that thrives on injustice, individualism and the frustation of real human needs.

Thoreau's statement that the 'mass of men lead lives of quiet desperation' is more true today than in 1849, while women's oppression ignored by Thoreau continues in both new and traditional forms.[38] The roots of alienation and despair are as much social and structural as personal and psychological. A society where the relationship of man to man, man to woman, parent to child is based on cash values is a barren one. Mrs Thatcher's much publicized statement 'that there is no such thing as society, only individuals' is borne out by the breakdown of traditional communities and our collective loss of meaning.

The notion of any kind of society, let alone a Green one, is alien to a whole class of politicians, marketing consultants, bureaucrats and media figures. If needs for community, friendship or affection can be turned into needs for more consumer durables, all the better. Soap operas about neighbours and communities are billion-viewer substitutes for real communities and real contact with one's neighbours. Work is often seen as boring, hierarchically organized and destructive. The education system looks more and more like a grand and pointless intelligence test to separate the managed from managers. Human misery is transformed into mass consumption, while we cannot buy happiness or creativity, comfort or companionship, we can buy another record, book or can of beer. The exploitation of sexual and other insecurities to sell goods that cannot compensate for such insecurities or meet real needs leaves us more frustrated and alienated. Capitalism has turned us into Marcuse's 'One-dimensional man'. Human beings have massive potential but a potential that is only seriously explored and developed as a means towards financial gain. Physically, intellectually and spiritually we may want to grow, but such growth is downgraded: it is not 'productive'.

A Green society, to be one where we can 'enjoy rather than feel restricted'[39] by material constraints, will have to make economics a tool for human growth rather than human beings a tool for economic growth. The myth of continued material progress has to be replaced by the reality of a dynamic self-managed, self-organized society where the difference between work and leisure is blurred, where community capital owned by neighbourhood groups allows us to produce our own clothes and tools and commodities if we so wish, and where good libraries, learning centres and sports facilities allow us to develop as human beings.

A Green society will have to be one where people do far more for themselves; where we are self-reliant enough to produce more of our food and housing on a decentralized level. At present we are encouraged to sit back – feeling powerless to change our surroundings and make decisions in the face of centralization and bureaucracy, we become apathetic. Often hating work, we consume as a form of compensation for our alienated labour and lack of any say over the form and content of our work. Essentially, we are rewarded if we are passive. Feeling socially or spiritually empty we attempt to fill the gap with material things, but it only becomes larger. 'Transforming a society of spectators into a society of activists is perhaps the greens' greatest challenge,' stated the *New Internationalist* magazine.[40]

Taking control of our lives may seem strange at first. We are usually more secure when led than when we lead ourselves. In 'liberating' us from an admittedly paternalistic welfare state, Mrs Thatcher took on the role of the nation's public-school nanny. Conservatism has become the fear of one's own shadow; the demand for a leader to hold hands and clean collective nappies. An imperfect welfare state will be replaced by something far more authoritarian. Although the fear of freedom will be strong, we will have to make our own decisions and co-operate with each other in an adult way, as part of a society shorn of hierarchy and sexist stereotypes.

There are a number of other obvious features of a Green society that follow on from the need for self-management and social justice. A redistribution of work will be just as important as a redistribution of wealth. We will share more. Power, violence and greed will still exist but be seen as vices to beware of rather than virtues to indulge in. Coca-colanization will give way to cultural diversity. A Green society would demand a Green attitude to crime, one going to the roots of the insecurities that drive people to crime through false or unfulfilled needs.

One difficult area will be that of defence. While much has been written on the practicalities of secure defence without offence with both social defence and purely defensive weapons being options up for debate, there needs to be discussion of what is to be done with existing armies. Would the British Army, let alone the much larger armies of France or the U.S.A., allow Green governments to function in peace? The answer is clearly uncertain given the experience of democratically elected governments from Spain in the 1930s to Allende's Chile in the 1970s toppled by military force. At least a partial answer comes from Peter Tatchell's book *Democratic Defence*[41] which explores the contradiction of how an institution as profoundly undemocratic and hierarchical as our present army is supposed to defend a 'democratic' system. While armed forces exist – and they will certainly exist in the transition – they will have to be linked strongly to the community, taking on a peace-making rather than war-fighting role and being involved in conservation work and ecological reconstruction.

An ecological order will also have to take a feminist form, where women do less of the hard and under-valued labour but get more of a say. Much of Green thinking, far from being automatically feminist, is dangerously sexist; it over-emphasizes women's nurturing parental role and its links to protecting the Earth, making women 'greener' but keeping them in a secondary position.[42] There can be no doubt that despite all the struggles of the women's movement we live in patriarchy, according to Cynthia Cockburn; 'Women constitute half of the world's population, perform two thirds of its work hours, receive one tenth of the world's income and own less than one hundredth of the world's property.'[43] A Green society if it deserves the title will have to end the sexual division of labour that penalizes and disempowers half the population. Childcare will need to be more collective and more community orientated both to allow women more space and allow individuals to grow up without over-dependency and isolation. Crèches and nurseries would have to involve men in bringing up children. Patriarchy will have to be taken up by the roots.

A Green education will have to involve not just the five-to sixteen-year-olds but allow for all of us irrespective of age to continue learning throughout life. There are surprisingly few descriptions of a Green education and it is an area where the advocates of small schools based in the community battle with the no-school supporters of Illich's *Deschooling Society*. In his novel *Island*, Huxley filled in the details of a Green education while illustrating that to reach a Green society we will have to make explicit the links between humanity and nature:

> Never give children a chance of imagining that anything exists in isolation. Make it plain from the very first that all living is relationship. Show them relationships in the woods, in the fields, in the ponds and streams, in the village and country around it. Rub it in . . . And let me add . . . that we always teach the science of relationship in conjunction with the ethics of relationships. Balance, give and take, no excesses – it's the rule in nature and translated out of fact into morality, it ought to be the rule among people . . . Treat Nature well and Nature will treat you well. Hurt or destroy Nature, and Nature will soon destroy you. In a Dust Bowl, 'Do as you would be done by' is self-evident – much easier for a child to recognize than an eroded family or village . . . Sand and gullies are parables. Confronted by them it's easy for the child to see the need for conservation and then to go on from conservation to morality – easy for him to go on from the Golden Rule in relation to plants and animals and the earth that supports them to the Golden Rule in relation to human beings. And here's another important point. The morality to which a child goes on from the facts of ecology and the parables of erosion is a universal ethic. There are no Chosen People in nature, no Holy Lands, no unique Historical Revelations. Conservation morality gives nobody an excuse for feeling superior or claiming special privileges. 'Do

> as you would be done by' applies to our dealings with all kinds of life in every part of the world. We shall be permitted to live in this planet only for as long as we treat all nature with compassion and intelligence. Elementary ecology leads straight into elementary Buddhism.[44]

Who knows whether a Green society will measure up to Huxley's Utopia or whether such a reliance on natural morality would have its own dangers?

## Another green world?

Having examined the need for a Green society to work within various criteria it is worth briefly summarizing some of its main features.

A starting point will be to define human worth in terms other than pounds and dollars; replacing the measurement of GNP with indices of human and ecological health and happiness. Needs will be critically examined and greed discouraged. Economic activity will cease to be an end in itself. Decentralization will be vital, both as a way of reducing energy consumption and of giving communities more autonomy. Local production for local use will be the norm. There will be less formal work, although the pursuit of leisure and play will increase. Technology will be assessed ethically as well as economically before being introduced. Renewable energy sources will displace both fossil fuels and nuclear power. Fewer goods will be manufactured, those that are produced in old-fashioned factories will last longer. Addictive consumerist hype will disappear. Advertizing will shift from persuading to informing. Farming will go organic and wisdom will replace chemical warfare in the cultivation of crops. Medicine will become holistic, tackling mental, physical and social factors, so as to keep us healthy and happy on less than the present NHS budget. Parish councils will levy taxes at a local level. National, regional and maybe even global legislatures will act to referee economic and social justice, using 'rate support grants' where appropriate. Society will start treating women like human beings. Education, Huxleyian or otherwise, will stress human rather than commercial values, encouraging individuals to define and develop their own potential. Human progress will no longer spiral upwards on a mountain of discarded rubbish and broken toys but move in new directions – inwards and outwards.

Of course a Green society will be flawed, just as are all possible human societies. Perfection is after all boring, unnatural and leaves no space for growth. There will be contradictions. Decentralization may collide with wealth inequalities and environmental controls. Greens will continue to disagree, but a Green society will work only within the broad parameters of social justice, self-management and sustainability. These minimum criteria are beyond ethical and political debate. Nothing else will work. Without a redistribution of wealth and responsibility, the great mass of the population will never put up with ecological restraints that lead to a fall in the 'standard of living'. If we cannot live within biological limits, we will either cease to live or cease to live as human beings; the former being the more likely possibility, while the latter is catalogued precisely and grotesquely by Huxley in *Brave New World*. The real challenge will be that of evolving into any of a number of possible different societies within these parameters. The Green movement will re-define politics as the art of *getting to* the possible. The problem, as we shall see in the next chapter, is that the solutions posed so far to the question of how we reach a Green society have been far from adequate,

Getting there won't be easy; it will demand massive political, structural, economic and above all psychological change over a long period of time. We must start to build the foundations now.

# 2
# Unfortunate solutions

*The Guardian* headline of 25 June 1988 warned of 'Pollution threat of scorched Earth' with a claim that 'Nasa scientist urges "cut the waffle" on danger of global drought'. A week later Geoffrey Lean in *The Observer* claimed that increasing $CO_2$ emissions would lead to dramatic warming: 'The last equivalent temperatures were at least 125,000 years ago when the climate was 2–2.5 degrees warmer, and elephants, lions and hippopotami roamed the Home Counties as freely as today's property developers.'[1] In fact hardly a day goes by without some mention of the greenhouse effect, the plight of the Black Forest or the dangers of nuclear power. Comment on how we might overcome these threats and move towards an ecologically sustainable society is rarer.

## Business as usual

One common response to the challenge has been to do nothing and claim that no action is necessary. Things are as green as they need to be. Nuclear weapons and power provide for national security. Poor countries should restrict their populations. There is no scientific evidence for acid rain. Every expense is spared. More research is almost always needed. Business continues as usual. Survival issues come second to strikes, inflation and the pursuit of every day politics.

'If trends are allowed to persist the breakdown of society and the irreversible disruption of the life-support systems on this planet, possibly by the end of the century, certainly within the lifetimes of our children, are inevitable,' warned *Blueprint for Survival* in 1972.[2] Having examined resource depletion, the problems of pollution, postulated overpopulation and ecological breakdown, an earlier panel of environmental experts concluded in the notorious *Limits to Growth* report that continued economic growth was impossible.[3] The authors of both reports were accused of hysteria and largely ignored. At the 1973 UN conference on the human environment government representatives stated that they did not 'believe that international controls and management of the environment are necessary, at least for the present.'[4] *The Global Report to the President* warned, 'If present trends continue the world in 2000 will be more crowded, more polluted, less stable ecologically and more vulnerable to disruption. Despite greater material output, the world's peoples will be poorer in many ways than they are today.'[5] Commissioned by Carter, it was shelved by Reagan. The final statement of the World Commission on Environment and Development headed by Geo Harlem Brundtland, the Prime Minister of Norway, claimed that very great care will have to be taken '. . . to ensure that human progress will be sustained through development without bankrupting the resources of future generations' and called for urgent action.[6] Five years later neither Britain nor America had made any official response.

Lip service comes before real concern East and West. A CDU party worker in Baden-Baden during the 1987 election campaign claimed that there was no serious pollution in West Germany; that if there were, the cause was from other countries; and that the Christian Democrats were best qualified to deal with it if it became a problem (which it wasn't).[7]

The situation is even worse in the 'socialist' countries, yet, to take one example, ecology is enshrined in the Russian legal system. Article 18 of the Soviet constitution states that 'In the interests of the present and future generations, the necessary steps are taken in the USSR to protect and make scientific, rational use of the land and its mineral and water resources, and the plant and animal kingdom, to preserve the purity of air and water, and ensure production of natural wealth, and improve the human environment.'[8] Article 67 continues, 'Citizens of the USSR are obliged to protect nature and conserve its riches.' Such warnings did nothing to prevent Chernobyl or the earlier Celiabinsk nuclear explosion, while discharges of sulphur and nitrous oxides from Russian factories have devastated the forests of Czechoslovakia and Poland.[9] Despite such disasters pre-glasnost party officials have been able to claim that 'universal ownership of the means of production and of all natural resources fore-ordains the successful resolution of ecological problems in the USSR.'

A variation is to cut out any such justification and mention the word 'green' as often and as loudly as possible. Thus even Mrs Thatcher can claim to be 'a friend of the Earth', while headlines proclaim politicians as varied as Presidents Reagan, Bush and Gorbachev as 'Green'. If action is needed it is best left up to 'us your elders and betters', cry the bureaucrats, the PR men and politicians the world over.

## Eco-capitalism

Wilfred Beckerman, a keen pre-Thatcher Thatcherite, argued that 'a price mechanism solution rather than a direct control method' associated 'with Soviet-type economies' was the answer.[10] Leaving it up to supply and demand is an approach allied to socialist optimism. Free enterprise ecology that ranges from the polluter pays principle through to bizarre plans for whale privatization is on the agenda. Milton Friedman has pushed the idea of making private enterprise pay for pollution through taxation, so as to allow the market to cleanse the biosphere. The Thatcher government believes that energy can best be saved through privatization and increased cost to the consumer. The Reaganite economist Julian Simon has claimed that if habitats have any economic value, they will be preserved without the efforts of environmentalists, however well meaning. In a similar vein James Watt, then Republican Secretary of the Interior, suggested that oil exploration and mineral extraction should be encouraged in America's national parks.

The answer to resource scarcity is supposedly the market. As oil runs out, it will become more expensive encouraging consumers to cut back, while giving entrepreneurs an added price incentive to prospect for new reserves and develop alternatives from shale to sugar cane. In fact many economists have argued that oil and gas need never run out in any real sense and that resource taxes can help the process of conservation along, while new reserves of energy are developed.

Such arguments that extend free market mechanisms are seductive. Every Green Party in Western Europe has a manifesto commitment to resource and pollution taxes. Third World debts are being swapped for rainforest conservation deals. *The Green Capitalists: Industry's Search for Environmental Excellence* by John Elkington has endorsed the market mentality.[11] David Owen, the British leader of the Social Democrats, proclaims the social market and the linked concept of Green economic growth. Sustainable growth – the marriage of economics and ecology – is a potent and popular concept.

Critics argue that left to its own devices the market can never get us to a Green society. If one taxes pollution why not tax murder and rape as well? Surely prevention is better than regulation. Given the incentives toxins will still be spewed out and dumping will continue. As energy reserves and mineral deposits deplete they will become expensive. But the cost won't be just economic. More Indians will be herded of their reserves, more areas of wilderness lost, more seas polluted. The Earth will be squeezed dry for a few more drops of oil.

Poverty is a source of frustrated destruction particularly when peasants are pushed off land used to grow cash crops, so as to exploit fragile and marginal land. Unfettered free enterprise looks unlikely to redistribute between rich and poor, feed the starving or bring real global prosperity. The market has no way of separating out real needs from mere whims backed up by dollar, lira or rouble. Increased oil prices will act as a global poll tax, causing the most discomfort to those living on least, while in relative terms sparing the well off.

Despite Beckerman's claim that '. . . the "poverty" argument against charging is not even true, since the pollution is caused by industry and the charges would be borne by people with higher incomes,'[12] oligopolies (of which the oil industry is a text book example) would be able to put their prices up and pass on the tax burden to the customer. Such indirect taxes are always regressive. In other words, the poorer the person the greater the proportion of income they pay. Ecology could be just another disguised justification for reducing welfare and public services, while shifting taxes towards those least able to pay.

Multinationals may hoard strategic metals and vital minerals as resources are depleted, increasing profit and political influence. They already control seed stocks. They will soon control governments. It is unlikely that crop strains that swallow less energy in the form of pesticides and fertilizers will be encouraged by oil producers. The existence of such multinationals gives the lie to the idea of a truly free market, made up of dozens of ferociously competitive firms, who through their antagonism and weakness give consumers sovereignty. The free market doesn't exist, never has and never will. Even if it did, it would be unlikely to solve our problems. It is clear that the pursuit of profit is a cause of, not a cure for, environmental damage.

## Gaia to the rescue

James Lovelock's Gaia thesis that the entire planet works as a giant life-support system, briefly touched on earlier, has been used as another justification for inaction; whatever damage we do to the Earth, Gaia will naturally make it good. If Gaia in her most robust manifestation seems so much more powerful than puny humanity, we should not worry our naïve heads about ecological problems. Anything we do is akin to kicking sand at the sun; 'If by pollution we mean the dumping of waste matter there is ample evidence that pollution is as natural to Gaia as is breathing to ourselves and most other animals.'[13] Ozone depletion, for example, was rejected as near impossible by Lovelock because volcanoes have put out the equivalent of millions of tonnes of ozone thinning aerosols throughout history without doing major damage. In turn Gaia maintains the Earth's temperature at an optimum for life and will respond to changes in temperature by altering atmospheric gases to get back in balance. Whatever we do Gaia through sophisticated but healing feedback mechanisms will eventually put right.

Since Lovelock wrote *Gaia* the ozone layer has thinned above the Arctic and there is hole above the Antarctic. The concentration of carbon dioxide in the atmosphere has increased and temperatures are now rising. It is clear that biological processes can adapt to massive external change, but it is less clear that they can adapt rapidly. We are producing $CO_2$ far faster than natural systems can mop it up. Extinction is a biological law, but with so many species now under threat Gaia faces a very great challenge. The interactions between biological and social systems are as important as Gaia's internal mechanism. One wonders what Gaia's response has been to former President

Marcos, who cut down over half of the Philippino forests with the help of US backers.[14] As Lovelock notes,

> the brutal disturbance of natural ecosystems always involves the danger of upsetting the normal balance of atmospheric gases. Changes in the production of gases such as carbon dioxide or methane and of aerosol particles may all cause perturbations on a global scale. Moreover, even if Gaia is there to regulate and modify the consequences of our disruptive behaviour, we should remember that the devastation of the tropical ecosystems might diminish her capacity to do so.[15]

Coastal pollution increases and yet more eco-systems come under threat, the Earth's vital organs are being ripped out. We cannot afford to wait for Gaia.

## The technological fix

Technological fixes have been seen as another solution, both as a way of ameliorating the worst effects of industrial society and of moving forward to a new kind of society. Others though have called for the rejection of all technology.[16] Technology cannot be rejected. Could an Ecotopian blacksmith forge the hundreds of ball bearings needed for a 15-speed mountain bike or even a one-speed with solid tyres? Could the anti-technological *Green Anarchist* collective publish their journal without the aid of a typewriter and a creaky, hand turned Gestetner? Conservationists in the last century bitterly opposed the building of railways. If we are to remain within ecological constraints without having to live in poverty and misery, goods will have to be built to last longer, energy conservation improved and new non-fossil fuel sources of power developed.

The bulk of research in Europe and North America is funded by military or commercial interests. Science is far from value-free when financed by armies or multinationals. Too often we are made to fit in with technological progress rather than the other way round, biotechnology being potentially a frightening example. Industry should be made to work in the strict context of what is acceptable to human beings and the natural environment. Even when applied for purely altruistic reasons, technological fixes can have staggering side effects. The elimination of trypanosomiasis (a cattle disease) in the Sahel has indirectly extended the Sahara and rapidly accelerated desertification, by allowing the introduction of thousands of cattle. Solar powered irrigation in Arizona has depleted water tables. The use of canals for similar irrigation in fourth millennium Sumeria led to salinization, crop destruction and 'the satanic mockery of snow.'[17] The path to hell is paved with good intentions. Technology alone is not enough.

## The population bomb defused?

During the late 1960s and 70s many observers came to reject notions that technological fixes or the market could be trusted to solve the mounting problems of resource depletion, pollution and habitat destruction. Saying it didn't matter, or passively leaving things for government and UN agencies to sort out, was no longer sufficient. From the *Limits to Growth* through to the work of Edward Goldsmith of *Blueprint* fame, researchers claimed that continued economic growth was neither possible nor desirable; that fundamental changes had to be made. Radical questions led to conservative answers. With the exception of Professor Barry Commoner, ecologists identified population growth as a root cause of crisis. The call went up in the seventies that 'there is only one form of pollution . . . people.'[18] With Garrett Hardin, his lifeboat thesis, arguing that while it might be charitable to increase food aid (rescue survivors), this would merely encourage faster population growth (swarms of people trying to get on board), with the result that eco-systems would collapse (the life boat would sink).

> We may be tempted to try to live by the Christian ideal of being "our brother's keeper", or by the Marxian ideal of "from each according to his abilities, to each according to his needs." Since the needs of all are the same, we take all the needy into our boat, making a total of 150 in a boat with a capacity of 60. The boat is swamped, and everyone drowns. Complete justice, complete catastrophe.[19]

In the eighties some 'Deep Ecologists' have praised AIDS and the Ethiopian famine. Many saw the way forward in terms of culling the peoples of Africa, Asia and South America; some still do.[20]

Yet some people weigh more than others. Perhaps for every US passport holder chucked overboard, Hardin could have fitted in fifty Bolivians or eighty Eritreans. The real problem is not over-population but over-consumption and resource maldistribution. Most students of population dynamics now believe that poverty leads to over-population rather than the other Malthusian way round. Without the safety net of a basic income scheme or adequate pensions and unemployment benefit, large families are a form of life insurance. Goldsmith, also a supporter of population control, argued somewhat paradoxically that 'the greatest damage done by state welfare, however, is to bring about the disintegration of the family unit itself.'[21] Clearly the analysis of the Hardins, Ehrlichs and other population bombers was fatally flawed.

## A party without politics

Such over-simplifications were matched by incredible political naïvety. Politics was viewed as a diversion. The disputes between East and West and between different groups in society were seen as irrelevant in comparison to ecological realities. Questions of why a minority had first class tickets on spaceship Earth while many of the rest were forced to stow away in baggage, let alone of who would have a place in the escape pod, were left unanalyzed. These ecologists were blind to the links between global prosperity and poverty. They felt it was enough to propose solutions and allow governments to take them up. Politics was seen as a game. Ecology was seen as being above human conflict. Heilbronner argued that democracy was incompatible with ecological survival.[22] Hardin called for 'mutual coercion, mutually agreed upon'.[23] Nicholson dedicated his book, *The Environmental Revolution*, some what sinisterly to the 'New Masters of the World'. Naïvety led to authoritarianism.[24]

Within weeks of the publication of *Blueprint*, the rather more enlightened scientific commentator Sir Eric Ashby warned that the call for an ' "orchestrated" overall plan to compel people to adapt themselves to live in equilibrium with nature' was neither realistic nor feasible 'even for single nations, let alone the whole world' and that 'unless enforced by autocracy [*Blueprint*] is unlikely to get further than the drawing board.'[25]

Politics was largely replaced by wishful thinking and apocalyptic musing. *The Ecologist* compared the plight of late twentieth-century civilization with the fall of Rome. The social structure was crumbling and the institution of the family under attack. One might 'safely assume that these social deviations also characterized the depressed areas of urban Rome during the Later Empire,' wrote Goldsmith.[26] The electorate were seen as greedy, short-sighted and stubborn in their destructive love of materialism. Goldsmith called for a return to Palaeolithic tribalism. Others looked to a man who would reverse the Beeching cuts and make the trains run on time. Much of the explanation for the decline of the environmental movement in the 1970s can be seen in its failure to link ecology up with social issues or real human problems.

> The most glaring omission from '*A Blueprint for Survival*' is any discussion of how 'The Goal' set out is to be reached politically . . . The great danger of the Blueprint is that, precisely because of its political weakness, the ecological movement will like so many movements in the past blossom strongly only to fade away, leaving us to stifle in our own squalor.[27]

## The Greens

Gradually things changed and people looked for new solutions. In the US Friends of the Earth helped support the official Environmental Protection Agency and got involved with legal battles to save the environment. In France René Dumont stood in the French presidential election of 1974, taking nearly 1.5% of the vote on a radical programme:

> It is one and the same system which organises the exploitation of the workers and the degradation of living and working conditions and puts the whole earth in danger. The blind policy of growth which is so extravagantly praised by all political parties, takes no account of either human well-being or of the environment. In this system the costs of pollution, then of depollution are added together to swell the production

> figures, though in fact they cancel one another out. Goods with built-in obsolescence that deteriorate as soon they are bought, the wastes that accumulate, the production of armaments, the recourse to ever larger and more dangerous technology: our system has to run faster and faster in order to stay where it is.

Dumont proclaimed; 'But don't wait for things to change by themselves. Only you have the power to change them.'[28] Political ecology spread across Europe, with successes first in France, and with more permanence in Germany, where Die Grünen became the first new party to enter the Bundestag for thirty years. Such parties gradually pushed away the Edward Goldsmiths and Garrett Hardins. Flesh was put on to apolitical bones. Green analysis widened. The links between social injustice, international problems and the threatened biosphere were made clear. Support for embattled groups – the unemployed, Turkish immigrants and other 'guest workers', gays and lesbians along with inner city communities struggling for better conditions – became part of Green political practice.

But the Greens still have to face up to many of the dilemmas avoided by their predecessors. The solution is now seen almost exclusively in terms of electing governments and legislating for change. Yet even if the continental Green Parties could increase their support to upwards of 30% and sweep into parliaments, even if Britain and America had fair electoral systems, such a strategy would be far from adequate.

## The parliamentary road to Ecotopia

Political ecologists who see a smooth transition to Westminster would do well to examine the experiences of Britain's co-opted and crushed Labour governments. The MacDonald administration of the 1920s degenerated into conservative National Government. Attlee pushed forward the programme for nuclear weapons and built the first atomic power stations to fuel them. Harold Wilson supported Nixon in Vietnam. Tony Benn, knowingly or otherwise, imported uranium from South African occupied Namibia. Denis Healey pre-empted Mrs Thatcher by introducing monetarism, three years before her first election victory. Neil Kinnock's front bench somehow managed to vote for clause 28. The media savaged Kinnock over unilateralism and gay rights. Tony Benn claims to have been misled by his civil servants. Attlee had to gain and maintain US support, MacDonald had to water down and ultimately ditch a socialist programme in order to build a parliamentary block large enough to govern. The International Monetary Fund held a gun to Healey's head.[29] It would be *more* difficult for the Greens.

A Green government would face the ferocious lobbying of special interest business groups. Wapping and, in Germany, the Springer Press would go for the Green jugular, producing tales of ministerial corruption and backbench fornication. The wrath of the US government would present another challenge. The need to form a bloc with traditional parties and to maintain electoral support in the face of radical economic and social change would grey the contents of any Queen's speech. Permanent secretaries would continue, while impermanent elected Greens would be very much at a disadvantage. Greens would not so much be corrupted by power as confined by impotence. The medievalness of Westminster would wilt any radical challenge and the German Bundestag has proved just as debilitating for Green parliamentarians. In Chris Mullin's *A Very British Coup* a moderately socialist prime minister faces everything from capital flights to armed insurrection.[30] Yet the policies enshrined in the relatively centrist British Green Party manifesto would make Harry Perkins (the book's Labour Party hero) a far more conservative Prime Minister than any Jonathon Porritt. Any Green government will be under heavy and unrelenting pressure.

## The Green revolution

The revolutionary left reject any such parliamentary path to eco-socialism. They say that constitutional democracy is a façade for rule by multinationals. Power is hidden from politicians. Real politics is found in class formations. The present system cannot be reformed, they say, but should be changed through revolutionary struggle.

Marx and Engels made a clear distinction between 'utopian' and 'scientific' politics. The utopians such as Saint-Simon, Owen and other Green forefathers had no strategy with which to move forward towards a different kind of society. The deficiencies of the utopians, who felt that change could be brought about through argument and education alone, without attacking class power and economic domination directly, were made crystal clear by Marx. Almost word for word the same criticism might be addressed at the Greens. Changing structures has to be more important than piecemeal lifestylism. Marx argued that change could only come through a working class revolution made inevitable through the contradictions of capitalism leading to ever increasing poverty, unemployment and the division of the community into mutually hostile groups; the proletarians versus the bourgeoisie. Such thinking has itself proved utopian.

In the sense that economic imperatives of capitalism contradict the long term biological conditions necessary for the continuation of human life – and in this sense alone – Marx's socialism could be termed scientific. But Western society has become wealthier in many ways and the interests of the worker have been confused with that of the boss. Some commentators see a global ruling class composed both of 'capitalists' and pampered workers lording it over an impoverished 'third world' working class from whom they extract surplus value. Economic growth has become a new opium of the people. Marxism is in a sense a form of Victorian New Ageism – the workers show no more sign of spontaneous uprising than the harmonic convergences at Glastonbury and other sacred sites do of coming together to save us. Marxism has for many become a new form of mysticism, a new slice of pie in the sky to be served up tomorrow.

The end of the expectation of inevitable revolution led to the manufacturing of a Leninist alternative whereby a small secretive party of trained cadres acted as a 'vanguard' to push things forward. The likelihood of such a storming of the Winter Palace in Britain or elsewhere in Western Europe, let alone worldwide, is remote. The revolution foreseen by Marx is a hundred years overdue and time is slipping away. Given the environmental contradictions of capitalism, tomorrow may be too late.

The notorious dogmatism and the conservatism of the Leninist left is equally problematic. The fraught and complex relationships between men and women, human beings and nature, people and technology are reduced to economic categories: 'It should be obvious that a society based on social ownership and control of the means of production would be better able to avert and/or cope with environmental disasters.'[31] If only life were so simple. The old-fashioned Left's uncritical support for capitalist economic growth that counts built-in obsolescence, cancer operations and Chorleywood processed loaves of Mother's Pride into G.N.P. is identical to that of their free market enemies. Ignoring the links between fossil fuels and the greenhouse effect *Socialist Worker* argues that 'it is precisely new scientific and technical advances, linked to and dependent on economic growth, that are required to avoid and, if need be, deal with the effects of planet warming. For example, *sea walls for protection against rising sea levels are themselves massive industrial projects.*'[32] Margaret Thatcher couldn't have put it better. There are other socialist solutions to the problem of getting to a Green society. But the more creative groups remain small and scattered. The *Marxism Today* style of Euro-communism seems in danger of sliding into centrism and consumerism, while remaining peripheral to the political mainstream. Anarchist and libertarian socialists do offer positive alternatives but despite a much longer history remain tiny in comparison to the Green parties. However *Green Anarchist*'s pro-Stonehenge and anti-technological politics aren't enough.

Traditional forces have largely hidden their heads in the sand. The Left has retreated into clichéd answers that didn't even address the old questions. The Greens have hardly begun to address the problem. The question of how we reach a Green society lacks well thought out solutions however skeletal or cautious.

# 3
# Structure

Is the future feasible? Is it possible to maintain prosperity without destroying global biological systems? Will the taps still supply water and homes remain warm, while the greenhouse effect is combatted and nuclear power phased out? Can we feed 56 million UK citizens and an ever growing world population without the environmental expense of artificial fertilizers and pesticides? In essence, what technical and structural changes will have to be introduced to make the future sustainable?

Answering such questions will be extremely difficult. We simply do not know what is sustainable. Establishing with certainty what can and cannot be done without disrupting the basic life support systems will demand a very different approach to scientific research from that pioneered by Bacon and Descartes in the seventeenth century. Science has been good at dissecting out linear truths – establishing which compound will be produced if two chemicals are made to react – but less good at working in a holistic way. We can calculate that A plus B will lead to situation C; ecological events where changes in A cause factors B to Z to change, some reinforcing the initial reaction and others damping it down, some biological and others social, are far more difficult to pin down. The greenhouse effect, fuelled by increased levels of $CO_2$, encourages plant growth that in turn tends to mop up the excess gas, yet as ice caps melt, darker areas of the Earth's surface will be uncovered and more heat from the sun absorbed, reinforcing the potential damage. Cutting down the rainforests and polluting the seas will make it more difficult for natural systems to regulate and remove the greenhouse gases: increased flooding will drive human habitation inland and into areas of former wilderness causing further greenhouse-fuelled deforestation. To predict let alone tackle these and other more complex feedback mechanisms will be no easy task. A Greener science will have to be more, not less advanced than the kind of research we have at present; a science that unites the study of natural phenomena with the human sciences of psychology and sociology, along with an investigation into networks as opposed to merely linear chains of causation. Cybernetics, ecology, quantum physics and mathematics will all furnish the tools necessary for the job. The future history of such a science is beyond the scope of this book but both mechanistic oversimplifications and vague mysticisms can be rejected.

## Using less energy

Even without such a revolution in research, some things are obvious. We will have to use a lot less energy and far fewer resources whether mineral or biological. Fossil fuels cannot be burnt on a sustainable basis, nor can we produce any appreciable amount of energy from nuclear fission or fusion without dire results. Even 'clean' energy sources produce environmental dirt. Windmills would lose much of their attraction if they became our sole sources of energy with a hundred on every hill and eight on every substantial building. Hydro-electric dams are already a major source of energy but are far from uncontroversial; the weight of water stored by dams may lead to earth tremors. Projects in the Amazon threaten to flood millions of hectares of rainforest, displace tribal groups and lead to the direct extinction of numerous plants and animals. The construction of the Aswan Dam in Egypt slowed the Nile and encouraged the spread of bilharzia, a disease produced by snails that live in sluggish water. Neither tidal barrages nor dams can produce energy in a truly sustainable form because they eventually silt up and while dredging may or may not be feasible for some rivers, it will hardly suffice for whole estuaries like the Severn or Mersey for which large barrages have been proposed. While rejecting earthquake-inducing giants small dams and water wheels could be used to produce energy without scarring the landscape or threatening ecological cycles.

Direct production of solar electricity through photoelectric cells is at present still too expensive to be viable but costs have come down ten-fold in a decade. One advantage is that once installed, cells require little or no maintenance allowing average costs per unit of energy to fall continually over the long life of a unit. Eventually, sunnier regions of the world from California to Kenya might produce much of their energy in a decentralized fashion directly from the sun. Even in Britain the skies are clear enough to produce some solar electricity on roughly half the days of the year. Passive solar heating costs nothing, and the siting of buildings so that they face the sun and trap solar energy with large windows could easily be encouraged through changes in planning regulations.

When and where the sun isn't shining, wind power is likely to be viable. With little in the way of technological innovation, a large fraction of Britain's energy needs could be met with wind farms sited in the North Sea. Small domestic windmills might be used to encourage local energy production. While massive tidal barrages present considerable dangers, smaller amounts of energy might be produced through wave generation without destroying marine eco-systems, disrupting the habits of wading birds, silting harbours or reversing tidal flows.

Biomass or energy from renewable biological sources could be produced in a variety of ways. Considerable areas (thousands of miles of hedges and park boundaries for a start) could be coppiced to produce a sustainable source of fuel wood. Coppicing involves cutting back the branches of fast growing trees like hazel, birch or alder to produce increased growth. Coppicing would lead to no net production of $CO_2$ because any $CO_2$ produced burning wood could be absorbed by newly growing staves in hedges. A variety of sources of organic waste could be tapped for methane, used to produce alcohol for public transport or burnt directly. Energy crops might be valuable with sunflowers and other fast growing species being used to produce food items and fuel at the same time.

Geothermal energy obtained by tapping the natural heat of the earth would also have a part to play. Already supplying much of Iceland's energy needs it is being developed in locations as diverse as Nicaragua, California and Cornwall. According to the Network for Alternative Technology and Technology Assessment geothermal sources could produce the energy equivalent of burning 4 million tons of coal in Britain alone by the year 2000 given the right support.[1] There may be drawbacks:

in Christopher Priest's novel *A Dream of Wessex*,[2] a large chunk of southern England becomes detached from the mainland after attempts to harness geothermal energy leads to geological instability and massive earthquakes!

It would be possible to discuss many more forms of renewable energy; all have drawbacks but a collective, complementary strength. Relying on any one source alone is likely to result in energy shortages, uncertainty and ecological damage. We must move towards a broadly based and diverse system of energy production. *No single source of energy will fulfil all our needs in a sustainable fashion.* The trick will be to phase out first nuclear energy and then fossil fuels, while introducing a mix of renewables. Initial costs will be high; many sources of renewable energy demand considerable capital investment but none involves the massive long-term costs associated with decommissioning nuclear power stations or clearing up the damage caused by fossil fuels that make such traditional forms of energy production uneconomic as well as unecological.

At present large amounts of energy are lost by transmitting electricity through the national grid along wasteful lines of pylons: it would be good to banish these eyesores that buzz angrily and are thought to cause maladies ranging from migraine to cancer. But banishing the national grid and producing energy in as decentralized a form as possible will also be difficult. Some areas would find it difficult to produce even a fraction of their energy needs in a renewable fashion and even where local energy production for local use was possible, some co-ordination would be vital. All renewable energy sources fluctuate; some days there is no wind, photoelectric cells are far from effective at 11.00 at night. Sophisticated computer switching mechanisms would need to mix and match sources of energy as the strength of solar, water and wind generated energy fluxed; back-up generators running on wood gas or alcohol would be necessary to guarantee a smooth supply. Storage is probably the greatest challenge. While solar or wind energy can be used to recharge batteries or transformed into other forms of energy resource, such processes are far from efficient.

The so-called fifth fuel is of course conservation. Even with a massive expansion of renewable energy production, we will have to use a lot less. Decentralization will save energy in a whole host of ways. Cheap public transport will have an obvious role. Combined heat and power schemes (CHPs) will pump round the excess heat from power stations through the radiators of nearby homes. Community laundrettes and other free or cheaply provided facilities will reduce our need to buy energy-intensive consumer durables. Electrical appliances can be made to use far less energy than at present. As already noted, goods can be made to last, repaired with economic standardized parts rather than scrapped, and finally recycled at the end of long working lives – saving huge quantities of energy at every stage.

Rather than forcing people to cut energy and resource use through coercion, the transition to an ecological society would work by making it easier to be Green, changing structure whether fiscal or physical so that individuals might be able to act ecologically without discomfort. In *Abandon Affluence!* Ted Trainer lists a whole series of items that we could lose or cut back on without any great suffering:

> We could easily make enormous savings in per capita resource use by cutting out unnecessary and wasteful production. Just imagine the savings that might be made if we did without the following things: a) ceased producing all frivolous luxuries and trinkets that anyone can do without, the sports car, furs, door-chimes, room-fresheners, hair-driers; b) cut right back on the things we rather like but could easily consume in far smaller quantities, such as liquor and soft drinks, cosmetics, magazines, confectionery and clothes; c) wore out old things; d) produced only a few simple models of most things, especially cars and household appliances; e) designed these items to be durable, to be repaired at home and to be easily re-cycled; f) eliminated all sources of inflated 'value-added' (the advertising that makes 3c worth of grain into a 69c packet of breakfast cereal); g) forgot all about fashion change; h) made an effort to refrain from buying things that would make little difference to our comfort and convenience; i) shared and hired many of the things that we used only occasionally; j) saved materials and used returnable and re-cycled items; k) were satisfied with what was functionally adequate, comfortable and convenient.[3]

Perhaps cars are the best example of an item that at present most of us feel that we could not do without but which will have to take on a very much reduced role in the future. Cars use up ridiculously large quantities of resources, accounting for over 10% of global trade in manufactured goods.[4] Motor vehicles generate more than 80% of carbon monoxide emissions; 51% of nitrogen oxides; 45% of hydrocarbons; 8% of particles and 3% of sulphur oxides. Over 10 million of the 30 million cars produced annually are driven in North America but the Chinese are planning to build a million a year from the late 1990s and are investing $10 billion dollars in the industry. Other 'Third World' countries would like to follow. Yet even maintaining a fraction of the hundreds of millions of vehicles already in existence looks to be impossible. They already use up 65% of all oil consumed in the United States and 44% in Western Europe. Every drop of oil has to be tortured out of the ground using huge amounts of water, solvents and salt solutions that pollute the environment and encourage earth tremors. We could find technical answers to a myriad of other car-created problems but lean-burn engines, catalytic converters, smaller cars and nicer oil companies will only make matters worse by allowing us to ignore the essential fact that there are too many cars which we use too often.

Structural change will be vital to help wean us off the car. Good public transport, good local services, better facilities for pedestrians and cyclists, together with user-friendly streets that discourage traffic, will be far more useful than simplistic, ignorant calls for us all to give up the car tomorrow without support. Psychological ties will be harder to overcome than the physical problems of getting from A to B. Emotional ties towards our protective, personalized, shiny transit shells will be difficult to break. Commuters still travel around London by car in spite of congestion so severe as to limit the average driver to a speed of just 6 miles per hour, far slower than cycling! If trends continue, such commuting will soon become slower than walking, yet millions of individuals still travel into the metropolis in their slow but private vehicles. We are socialized into loving the car and a thousand other consumer durables. Such socialization is a product of advertizing and structural factors that make giving up the car difficult in both practical and psychological terms for many people. The all-powerful road lobby that has the cash to convince the government that eight-lane motorways are a better solution to traffic problems than improved rail links, will fight the Greens mercilessly. Already a Swiss Automobile Party has had members elected to challenge the Greens.[5]

Rubbish is a number one source of pollution and a sink of energy that demands plugging. Much rubbish is unnecessary. It would be easy to cut excess packaging and abolish built-in obsolescence. Glass containers could be made returnable, non-biodegradable materials could be phased out, unrecyclable packaging such as drinks cartons built up of layers of plastic, aluminium and card abolished. Plastics which will not easily degrade can be burnt but leave a deadly residue unless incinerated very carefully and at very high temperatures. So-called biodegradable plastic creates non-biodegradable pollution from dioxins. According to *New Internationalist*, 'Two pounds of hazardous waste are produced for every pound of plastic.'[6] Plastics constructed out of simple organic blocks derived from ethylene (in turn based on alcohol from fuel crops instead of petroleum) would cut toxins and secure us from a future full of undead supermarket bags at the same time. What little rubbish was produced could be separated at source into small compartmentalized bins provided by local authorities with space for organic waste (which could be digested for methane and then used as fertilizer), metals, paper and card plus broken glass. Small fines (for householders) and large ones (for industry) could be used to ease the transition. Up to 98% of domestic refuse could be recycled economically.[7]

Sewage, instead of being mixed with heavy metals and other forms of industrial waste, might be pumped into farm gas units and tapped for methane. Burning off naturally-occurring methane from sewage and old rubbish dumps would be an excellent means of reducing the production of one of the worst greenhouse gases and getting energy out at the same time. Digested sewage would then make an effective fertilizer. The best way of reducing the production of toxic industrial pollutants would be to reduce industrial output by producing less. Clean water will be created not by new investment and better technology but by ending the use of artificial fertilizers and pesticides along with major cuts in industrial pollution. Water conservation and the recycling of grey water from washing to flush toilets within homes would reduce the need for new reservoirs that eat into the environment. Many buildings could, with simple changes, collect their own water (for uses other than drinking) at little expense.

## A new diet, a new agriculture

It would be possible to feed Western countries without cheap cash crops, artificial fertilizers or pesticides. A move to a more vegetarian diet would allow us to make much better use of the land and reduce our dependency on foodstuffs from the 'Third World'. The idea that vast tracts of upland Britain are fit only for sheep is largely a myth. Sheep and goats degrade land so as to make it fit only for sheep or goats; areas like Dartmoor and the North Yorkshire Moors were clothed with broad leaf woodland but deforestation robbed them of soil and livestock prevented them from being recolonized by pioneering and soil-enriching shrubs.[8] Freed from livestock, such areas would gradually be colonized by pioneer species like hazel and birch that would build up humus and make the land eventually fit for crop production. Large scale deciduous tree planting could be used to restore such land and replace coniferous plantations that acidify soils. New forests could be used to produce coppiced wood for burning or conversion into ethanol with no net increase in $CO_2$. Urban areas could also be reclaimed for organic agriculture; Trainer has argued that large areas of waste land in cities and towns might be converted into allotments and city farms to produce food. In the last war Britain survived enemy blockades and was virtually self-sufficient, so it can be done.

By working with nature we can maintain high yields and reduce energy inputs. Diversity is the key. Consumer capitalism requires uniformity even in vegetables; genetically engineered radishes which can be harvested in one morning, spring onions of the same length for hypermarket chains. The concern is with appearance and shelf life, taste is irrelevant. In the words of the song 'The public wants what the public gets.' Varieties that need plenty of pesticides and fertilizer are also favoured. Greens would revive local sub-species; carrots and potatoes that might look less attractive and homogenous but are better suited to local soil conditions and micro-climates; resistant to disease without high pesticide inputs. Monoculture exhausts the soil and breeds pests in the soil. Simple four-field rotation and intercropping of varieties that mutually repel each other's pests could be easily achieved.

Greens would go for diverse landscapes. On eroded hillsides in Mediterranean Europe and in similar climatic regimes (Britain after the greenhouse effect?), trenches can be dug into the unprotected bedrock, filled with earth and planted with olive trees that break up the limestone and create new sub-soil in the most arid conditions. Traditional 'slash and burn', despite a bad press, can be practised without destroying the rainforests as long as a number of large trees are left to grow, a diversity of indigenous crops are planted and the forest is allowed to recolonize after a number of years. A case study of the Kayapo in Brazil describes a system whereby:

> The clearings are managed for a number of years, first for annual crops such as maize, beans, squash and manioc, then for perennial and tree crops such as sweet potato (which can be harvested for five years), yams (five to eight years), papaya (five years), banana (fifteen to twenty years) and cupa (*Cissus gongylodes*) (up to forty years) . . . Old fields and secondary forest are particularly important for medicinal plants and as habitat for game . . . Fallow land is managed by planting useful trees, some of which take many years to grow to harvestable size.

The authors note that their research

> calls into question the apparent 'naturalness' of some existing tropical forests, and shows that a diversity of species and habitats can be maintained while yielding food, medicine and household products to their human managers. If the basic requirements of such a system – the systematic classification of soils and plants and the intensive management of second growth – are met, there is little to prevent the Kayapo's efficient and sustainable agriculture from being fruitfully applied in other parts of the world.[9]

Such forms of management that work with nature and promote diversity instead of monoculture can be applied in very different ecological zones. Pre-Columbian Mexico City was fed by enormously productive *chinampas* or floating gardens:

> What surprised and fascinated Bernal Diaz most was the 'agricultural' nature of the city he discovered. It was divided, on a grid system, by long canals intersected by river 'streets'. Between these 'streets' were rectangular plots of land with houses built on them. These were the *chinampas* . . . Constructing canals from the thick marsh vegetation, the Aztec people had piled up the surface vegetation like green 'mats'. Then, from the bottom of the canals, they had used mud to spread over the green 'rafts', which were anchored by planting willows all round them. The fertile plots that were constructed in this way produced a variety of crops, vegetables and fruit trees . . . Three harvests were possible, with transplanting from reedbeds; animals were kept and their manure (together with that of humans) used on organic gardens.

The canals also contained edible species of fish. The system which supplies the needs of a quarter of a million people could be mimicked to great effect all over the tropical regions of the Earth. Redclift, supplying the description above, notes: 'Perhaps an ecological alternative lies not so much in learning things we do not know as "unlearning" things we do know?' He made this statement after examining the pollution and poverty of twentieth-century Mexico.[10]

In more temperate areas, fully sustainable agriculture could use hedges for food and fuel, lakes and rivers for fish, water fowl and edible plants, exploiting the landscape ecologically without destroying it. Green planning and architecture would be vital. Houses have been designed and occasionally built that are so well insulated that they need no energy for heating. Simple changes in planning regulations could be used to encourage domestic and industrial energy production. Shared laundry provision and other community facilities could be created. Local development plans (decided democratically and directly by local populations) would include fishponds, compost heaps and urban meadows as well as light industrial units. The creation of ecological, cheap and long lasting housing could be encouraged through self-build schemes. The emphasis would be very much on the use of local building materials. The removal of all taxes both direct and indirect on building repairs would help to maintain buildings.

Ignoring for the moment the change in economics and belief

patterns that would make reduced consumption a major social goal, it is worth noting that some forms of 'green' structural change might act to reinforce unsustainable ways of living and over-consumption. 'Too many "alternative" investment ideas reinforce the existing structures, as for example the installation of district heating networks reinforces the concentration of the population in industrial conurbations.'[11] Bahro also notes that efficient public transport may encourage us to travel more and consume yet more energy. Yet Bahro also talks of abolishing railways, telephones and the microchip (I am not ashamed to have written this book on a wordprocessor!), while contradicting himself by saying that improved communication systems (via carrier pigeon?) would make travel unnecessary. Technology should be used carefully, not thrown away. Forcing people to stay in one place is nearly as bad as forcing them to commute miles to work every day. Bahro is naïve to see ecological change as a regressive phenomenon. The 'district heating networks' (presumably he means combined heat and power systems) that he also rejects could provide otherwise wasted energy to heat greenhouses, factories and housing estates without locking everyone into cities. The division between city and countryside could be positively eroded as urban areas become greened with city farms and the extension of allotments, making them attractive enough to reduce the desire for energy consuming escape. Run-down rural communities could in turn become viable through the decentralization of services like cinemas, libraries and community centres, so as to be pleasant to live in without the constant need to travel to larger centres.

Ecological changes have to throw up costs as well as benefits. Making things to last is both economically and ecologically good – it is a way of having our cake and eating it, of preserving both the hi-fi and the rainforest; but it will be expensive. A car that lasts fifty years will cost less than the next seven models necessary if it didn't, but it will cost more both in resources and in money than the usual model. Stringent standards for lower energy consumption and increased durability will have to be legislated for, and it may be necessary to introduce special low-interest credit arrangements so that buying the CFC-free fridge and the everlasting gas oven will be possible. The most serious drawback of making items to last longer will be that innovations which genuinely save energy, cut resource use or are superior in other respects will spread through society slowly if at all.

Motivation may be more of a problem than changes in technique or structure, whether in farming, energy production or resource use. A Green future will in actual fact be an off-white one; 100% recycled paper is grey, dioxin-free tea bags may be far from genteel, fruit and vegetables may look slightly blotchy. Fashion will become restricted and we will have to put up with the patched, the slightly grubby and the re-used. Many Americans are reluctant to spend more than fifteen minutes preparing a meal, so will they go to the trouble of separating their rubbish at source? Will taboos prevent the use of human sewage in farming? In a society with more leisure time and where women are no longer domestic slaves, this might be less of a problem. In a society which isn't orientated to economic growth, the financial gains from re-use will become more important, but the danger is that certain classes and individuals will attempt to establish their 'superiority' through old-fashioned conspicuous consumption. As it is, many individuals in the developing world seek to emulate our waste and luxury. How ever technologically feasible a Green society may be, such technology will have to meet popular acceptance.

## How to decentralize?

The decentralization process will demand some thought if it is to be painless and practicable. Within cities and in the countryside, work, housing and services would have to be re-combined in such a way that most journeys would become unnecessary. Regionalization would mean political power, the civil service, industry and cultural activities being federated away from the old capital cities. Many countries including the USA and USSR, India and China are already federated to a large extent and could be regionalized further without major problems. The situation will be more difficult in Britain or France where administration is concentrated in the capital cities with rail and road links radiating out of London and Paris. Given the huge quantities of blood spilt throughout human history over lines on maps, drawing up new ones will be far from easy. The concept of a bioregion, which bases decentralization around a biologically distinct region, may be of some value. But will a distinct biological area like a desert (!?), mixed farmland on granite soils, or deciduous forest belt contain the mix of features (including a port, major road and rail links and enough agricultural land to achieve relative self-sufficiency) to be viable? Perhaps a mixture of very different biological regimes might work more successfully as a distinct region. What of the areas where cultural and biological regions overlap but do not coincide? Or of units with strong historical identities that may well be too small or ecologically too uniform to function as effective and self-supporting regions? Surely the south-west of England could be made into a viable regional unit, but might not Cornwall (which has a much stronger cultural/linguistic tradition than neighbouring Wessex) be too small on its own? Bioregionalism could lead to nationalism and xenophobia: already the Estonian Green Party and other Green groups in the Baltic states are being used to support nationalistic and anti-soviet sentiments (which are understandable given the history of those peoples).

'Fourth Worlders' and other advocates of regionalism and cantonization can be just as reductionist in their perceived solution to ecological problems as the most vulgar of Marxists. Small is not always beautiful. Localized communities, far from being a panacea, are seen by many as closed, hostile and small minded; breeding grounds for racism, sexism and homophobia. Many people, especially the young, welcome the anonymity of cities as a means of escape. An ecological society would be highly unsatisfactory if all travel was restricted and individuals had no choice but to live in one acre all their lives. Society would indeed stagnate. The transition will only be possible if both cities and villages combine their best features while removing their worst. We need stronger communities but should avoid suffocation. At present the utility gained by those who value separateness is negated by the loneliness of those (particularly the old) who do not. Pluralism, especially the right of individuals to lead their lives in a variety of different ways, is as important as sustainability.

## Creating appropriate technology

What kind of technology fits human interests (and not just those of an elite) and works without disrupting natural cycles? Can technology be made to fit in with 'human nature'? Although human nature is a difficult and controversial concept, something largely socially conditioned rather than merely innate, we should at least try to make tools fit us rather than the other way around. Do we need to throw away our machines, retreat from industrialism or more modestly smash capitalism? Should technology be alternative, appropriate, radical or convivial; or all of these!? As we have seen, many ecological problems will demand technological advances; while we may reject industrialism as an ideology (in the sense of continual scientific and productive expansion as the answer to all questions), we cannot reject industry. While capitalism is obviously incompatible with sustainability, we should put capital under human control rather than naïvely trying to scrap it. At present the logic of capital means that an 'advance' has to be implemented whatever its costs, lest a rival company or country develops it first and swamps us with missiles or cheaper consumer goods.

Creativity would be better suited to developing technology within carefully developed constraints which attempt to define whether proposed innovations bring us real benefits that outweigh carefully assessed costs. Technology that enhances human skills and removes unpleasant, boring or dangerous work is more important than technology that produces further economies of scale for multinationals. One very important area is the need for technology that allows self-management and local production for local need. Many millions of words have been written on alternative technology, as on renewable energy, but dreaming of a Green society with fish and fountains, sunny afternoons in parks and geothermal energy is not enough. Green design is quite different from implementation. Along the way things tend to get lost. In *The Sun Betrayed* Ray Reece illustrated how benign, small-scale solar energy production was suppressed and hijacked by commercial and political power blocks.[12] The joint U.S. government and energy corporation plan succeeded, according to Reece, in controlling the development of solar energy, centralizing it, assisting major firms with subsidies, eliminating small firms and pushing for 'ungreen' high tech methods of production such as solar space ships. It is a 'story of deceit, vested interest, and collusion in the highest echelons of U.S. industry and government.'[13] Solar technology that worked but failed to provide multinationals with money or encouraged consumers to opt out of the grid was strangled at birth.

Getting good technology is more difficult than overcoming design faults. It isn't difficult to think of ways of making design and technology ecological; putting it into practice, though, is a political problem. Long before the dangers of CFCs from refrigerators were understood, there was a lively debate about which design of fridge would work best; gas adsorption or electric.[14] The gas adsorption model has many advantages: not needing a supply of mains electricity it would be an excellent way of helping 'Third World' communities to develop without an expensive grid, it is easy to maintain and cheap, it does not need CFCs, it has hardly any moving parts and is therefore quieter than its rival, etc. Its electric rival cost a massive $450 in 1923 and tended to break down regularly. But General Electric put a million dollars into research and development and pursued a vigorous marketing campaign which culminated in 1931 with the presentation of the millionth 'Monitor Top' to Henry Ford in a special radio broadcast. 'The machine that was "best" from the point of view of the producer was not necessarily "best" from the point of view of the consumer.'[15] Items are designed and sold not for our benefit or for that of the planet but instead only if they are expected to make a profit.

Some environmentalists have argued for authoritarianism, looking to dictatorships (benevolent or otherwise) or world governments. The botanist Sir George Stapledon naïvely asked for a global planned economy governed by conservative bureaucrats, 'the same type of man who had run the Indian Civil Service.'[16] Richard Gott, arguing from what sounds like a far right perspective (though this is in fact the voice of a Labourite trying to make the Greens out to be Fascists), claims that to solve our problems we will need the 'brutal and dictatorial powers of a Green Hitler, a Green Stalin, a Green Ayatollah, or even – the most recent of the Back to the Land visionaries in power – a green Pol Pot.'[17] On the contrary, we need to give people power over the technology and structures that shape their lives. Enabling people to make such choices will mean more than giving them power in the political sense: it also entails redistributing information at present wrapped up in secrecy laws and 'technical' jargon. Science needs to be seen as political; like the sources of power in our society it has been depoliticized and made invisible as far as the 'public' is concerned. An ecological perspective, which demands that we put usefulness and repairability before profit, can only be achieved by rejecting hierarchy and the concentration of power. The pursuit of power and the accumulation of capital by a few is a direct cause of our present crisis; further concentration of power whether benevolent or otherwise will only lead to more destruction. The issue is one of how power, information and the ownership of wealth can be redistributed. A Green future will also be a red one.

Technological development has far too often been in the hands of witch doctors and capitalists. Arthur C. Clarke, the science fiction writer and scientist, argued that 'Any sufficiently advanced technology is indistinguishable from magic.'[18] Such mystification is in the interest of practitioners like Mr Clarke who seek to preserve their dark powers by making them opaque to otherwise interested observers. Knowledge is after all power. When workers at the now famous Lucas Aerospace works were to be made redundant they wrote to 180 academics asking what they might do to retain their threatened jobs. They received four replies. Looking to themselves they came up with 150 product lines that could be produced with the then existing machine tools and skills! Yet all of these were rejected by the management as incompatible with existing product range; military aircraft were OK but kidney machines, carts to help children with spina bifida to walk, equipment to store energy from renewable sources and road-rail buses were not. The primacy of profit had its part to play in the downfall of the Lucas Plan but so did the mystification of science and the wholly artificial division of manual (low status) from mental (high status) labour. Workers are deskilled and reduced to robots while design and manufacture become ever more abstract from both human life and human labour. As Mike Cooley states:

> These design stages involve rarified, complex mathematical procedures which are necessary only because, for commercial reasons, materials and the systems of the product are designed just to perform a precisely defined function for a very short length of time before the product is rendered redundant (planned obsolescence). The rarified mathematical procedures are outside the experience of the mass of industrial workers

> and are used as a means of bludgeoning their common sense into silence.[19]

Local design centres could allow workers to thrash out technical and social problems associated with new products without such mystifications. Technology could be developed for use and not profit, motivating human creativity directly rather than through money. Workers (and consumers) should not just own the means of production, but carry out the research for new products in a democratic way.

But it is not sufficient to argue, as some left groups do, that there would be no technological problems in a society where the workers decided what to produce. Consumers need a say as well: what may create work and satisfy workers might still collide with wider social interest just as much as under capitalism. As we have already noted, technology, despite good intentions, often gives rise to negative and far-reaching consequences. Too often technology is used to try and solve problems created by earlier technical fixes. The effects of technology are social as well as ecological; the simplest of the structural changes described in this chapter will have enormous implications. Lynn White Jr. may have exaggerated when he claimed that the invention of the stirrup led to the fall of Rome (because the 'barbarian' hordes could remain on their horses while wielding sword and lance, enjoying an advantage over the Roman cavalry who could not) but he makes a telling point. It is far from deterministic to state that technology is not neutral. Centralized technology gives rise to centralized structures and vice versa. But decentralist, feminist, community controlled technology that is seemingly Green may give rise to unforeseen and occasionally unfortunate results. White describes the repercussions of the chimney:

> In the days of the old central fireplace, to keep warm in northern Europe everyone from lord and lady to humblest servant lived and ate together in the great hall, and slept there too, normally in curtained compartments. Society was hierarchical, but the strata knew each other intimately. With the new flexibility of heating made possible by chimney and mantled fireplace, privacy could be implemented. Lord and lady increasingly ate, lived, and slept in withdrawing rooms. As affluence increased, noble residences were redesigned so

> that rank after rank of the social structure could enjoy the new individuation in its life style. To Dresbeck's remark that the chimney may have affected the art of love more than the troubadours did, one may add that it may likewise have fostered the individualism of the later Middle Ages more than all the humanists.[20]

Wilde remarked that the kindest slave owners were really the most cruel because their slaves were less likely to seek freedom. Seen in this light we might argue that by making class antagonism clearer and smashing through sentimental bonds, the chimney gave birth to the fourteenth-century peasant revolts that rocked Europe. White is a reductionist and reduces social change to technological determinism but technology is not a neutral force and it does have social repercussions that should not be ignored.

At present we are a long way from being able to choose the kind of technology we want and preparing for even the unforeseen risks. Capital is still imprisoned by capitalists (or perhaps capitalists have been imprisoned by capital all along?); we have no control and the ownership of production is protected by the mystifications of 'scientific rationality'. But the productive process is often far from rational. For example, it is said that in the 1920s Henry Ford sent out a team of investigators to find the most common faults in the Model T Ford. They found a great many, in fact there was only one trouble-free component; the crankshaft. Ford ordered his designers to make it out of thinner metal. A Green future demands stronger crankshafts and many more difficult changes in technology, design and structure. These present problems but surmountable ones; a Green future is *technically* feasible. The question then is whether it is politically achievable. Will it be possible to overcome the Fords of today and tomorrow? This is a very much more vexatious question.

# 4
# Politics

A society that is ecologically sustainable, economically stable and socially just will demand political as well as technological change. Greens have to face up to the issues of power. Good intentions are not enough; if the world could be changed by argument alone political activity would be virtually unnecessary.

## Some obstacles to success

It could be argued that the Greens already have access to influence; Greens have been elected to national or regional parliaments in most European countries. Even in Britain there are over a hundred elected local councillors and the Party achieved a massive 15% slice of the vote during the 1989 European elections. There are large Green or at least environmental fractions within most traditional political parties from the German Social Democrats to the American Republicans. The most unlikely politicians, from Mrs Thatcher to Bush and Gorbachev, have been labelled 'environmentally conscious'. Non-party-political Green movements like Friends of the Earth and Greenpeace have millions of members worldwide and massive support. One can guarantee that from suburban Tokyo to rural Alsace local Greens will be meeting somewhere to plot election strategy, opposition to local development and direct action. The Greens are everywhere and are growing in strength.

But growth does not guarantee success. Greens are a long way from being able to influence let alone abolish the anti-ecological, growth orientated multinationals or to redirect national economies towards sustainability. Greens are marginalized by conventional political structures, traditional politicians claim with success to be environmentalists and label the likes of Petra Kelly and Joshkca Fischer as extremists. The pressure to appear moderate and drop radical policies (i.e. the ones that go to the roots of the ecological crisis) are enormous. The danger of a purely electoral approach is that it will create an outlet for frustrations and aspirations without changing society fundamentally. Elections and governments are a safe way of bottling up potential challenges to the system. Attempts to transform conventional politics from being 'more compensatory than emancipatory' threaten to split the Greens into numerous factions; fundamentalists (who reject all compromise but have no consistent theory of how to bring about change without it) and 'realos' (who would jettison fundamental policies in the hope of gaining 'influence' within the system), centralists who would use conventional structures and decentralists who believe the only way forward is through undermining and distributing power, life-style Greens, single issue campaigners, red, blue, dark and light Greens and many others. The purpose of this chapter is to try and assess where political power resides and how it can be used to create change by empowering a mass movement rather than a managerial elite.

Differences within the movement should be a source of strength rather than strife. Neither ideological uniformity nor organizational conformity should be seen as goals; pluralism has to be a first principle of a successful strategy that does not discourage individuals from getting involved. Different individuals have complementary skills and come from varied backgrounds and are bound to work most effectively if they do things in different ways. It may be a waste of time to convince Social Democrats that to be truly Green they must join a true Green Party. Party politics even in the most successful of Green experiments alienates many people who might prefer to take part in *ad hoc* direct actions or involve themselves with educational projects. A Green society will not be brought about purely through party political activity; every sector of society will need to be greened. Practical action, electoral politics, economic activity and ideological change will absorb different people. There is no true Green path because nobody however perceptive can predict exactly how a Green society will be brought about. A pluralist, non-dogmatic Green movement will allow the Greens to gain a collective strength difficult to achieve if all Greens were members of a single party hostage to fickle electoral fortunes. Political experiments will be necessary. Greens cannot afford to build a new church or split into dogmatic warring sects. Virtually every political or spiritual movement from the pre-Christian Essenes to the post-Stalinist Euro-Communists have proclaimed their message as 'The Message'. Such arrogance is a luxury that the planet cannot afford. In this sense Greens must be gentle to be effective.

Greens must be aware of the psycho-pathology of power, rejecting leaders and dogmas. All sorts of groups whether work-based, spiritual or social, tend to divide into hostile and opposed camps. The human race at least in present times seems to have a perverse need for enemies. Consciously or unconsciously, activists get involved for many reasons other than pure altruism. A shrewd attention to group dynamics and psychological factors is a prerequisite for any attempt to get to a Green world. Politics (party or non-party, formal or informal) can be hierarchical and alienating to women: feminist rhetoric and manifesto promises of women's ministries, nursery provisions and paternity payments must be preceded by a feminist political practice that rejects smoke-filled rooms, constricting agendas and male-dominated meetings. Before we can bring about political change, we have to tackle the personal in politics. Individuals cannot repress their egos, insecurities or need for false certainties, but they need to be constantly aware of the risks and motives.

There are signs of hope. At the final session of Die Grünen's 1988 conference all major sections of the party, the fundis, the realos, the left as curiously distinct from the eco-socialists, the feminists and the mothers, centrists and eco-libertarians were given a say. Despite some bitter battles, the party has its motto: 'Einheit in der Vielfalt' or unity in diversity.[1] Diversity though should not come at the expense of effective and coherent politics.

## Single issues are not enough

Some types of Green activity are more effective than others. At present most members of the Green movement prefer to put their efforts into single issue campaigns, working for conservation, disarmament or animal liberation. Yet such campaigns rarely tackle the root causes and are far from a good use of energy. For every whale saved, there are a hundred other species under threat. For every dictator who tortures and maims, many more are propped up by the CIA or the KGB. The seals saved from clubbing in the seventies are now dying from a virus, possibly linked to the dumping of PCBs.[2] Superficial reform is hard-won and counter-productive. Minor change takes the heat out of protest, while the forces of destruction grind on more quietly but no less dangerously. Campaigners should try to link up in a holistic way, working not just to slow the damage but to build something better.

Others seek such long term change through personal growth and individual action: 'Living more simply, that others may simply live'. Eating less meat or becoming a vegan, buying wholefood, going by bike or bus rather than by car are all part of this approach. If enough people were to join them, lifestylers argue, all our problems would be solved. Some call for a boycott of all 'Third World' cash crops, believing that the land in the south of the globe would be better used to feed the starving than to over-feed us. But will such non-consumption ever be taken up on a large scale? Might not personal action become a substitute for political change?

It is difficult to know how far such self sacrifices should go; vegan or just vegetarian, animal-free or avoiding synthetics which are by-products of the chemical industry, boycotting all goods from the 'Third World' or shifting to those that have been produced ethically. In the long run less international trade will mean less international exploitation but in the short run it might just mean more poverty for those who get at least a fraction of the monies from cash crops. It is impossible to promote land reform and social justice purely by not going to Sainsburys.

Despite such contradictions, personal change has its value. We have to experiment with ways of getting by which are more satisfying and less exploitative. There is nothing wrong with building alternatives now rather than waiting for the whole world to change with us. In the future, we will all have to learn to reduce our consumption of animal products, scarce resources and energy, so we might as well start practising now. In the words of Ted Trainer, we will have to 'Abandon affluence'.

Lifestyle change is popular. Throughout the 1980s vegetarianism was one of Britain's fast growing social trends; according to a Gallup poll in 1988 there were 13 million British vegetarians.[3] Carnivores are cutting back as well. The mountain bike has made cycling increasingly attractive. The peace tax campaign is growing in strength. Friends of the Earth even launched a Green Consumers' Week to make people think differently about a range of products from aerosols to Islay malt whisky. Politics need to be linked to daily life. But eating less meat in the hope that 'Third World' people will be fed, or switching to organic food so as to create a new agricultural order are acts of naïvety. It is unrealistic to believe that isolated individual actions multiplied many times over will change the world. The International Monetary Fund, the Common Agricultural Policy and the Ministry of Agriculture, Food and Fisheries all influence food production to a greater extent than the consumer. 'Lifestylism' can become a middle-class alternative to real action. For many, 'simple living' is a distant and incomprehensible luxury. Most working class families cannot get organic produce, would not be able to afford it and have until recently had little knowledge of its benefits. Labels still don't give us enough nutritional information to make proper choices and many poorer communities lack shops selling adequate food. Many people cannot do without cars and shouldn't be made to feel guilty because the bus station has been privatized, the village school cut or the corner shop replaced by an out-of-town hypermarket. The world won't be healed merely by people being nice to each other.

Green politics is about collective action. Personal change, heroic as it may appear to its exponents, is not enough. Individuals should surely support and empower each other. More can be achieved by groups working towards a common goal than by isolated individuals however enlightened. Getting together at weekends to clear waste land for collective allotments or helping with self-build housing schemes would be the kind of acts both practical and political that link people together, so that they can become strong. Green action isn't furthered by people shutting themselves away and dreaming they can do it on their own.

Rather than expecting ever greater sacrifices from the unwilling and the undeserving, Greens should aim to change structures so that living non-exploitatively becomes easier. Cycle ways and cheap convenient public transport, along with decentralized services, will reduce the need for expensive polluting private vehicles. Present subsidies on unhealthy food can be removed. Changes in the tax and benefit system could be used to create more flexible work patterns and encourage conservation. It is vital that we live simpler lives, cutting resource use and boycotting a whole host of products; but lifestyle change should be seen as a complement to, rather than a substitute for, structural political change.

## A Green political party

Others while accepting the need for structural change believe it can best be achieved through traditional political parties – that Greens would do best to join established parties and work within them. But Green politics is a distinct political philosophy, quite different from Conservatism, Liberalism or Social Democracy. It cannot be glued on; emerald tail feathers are not enough. Green ideas need to be argued for and worked for. Such values would always come second in any other grouping and the opportunity to persuade on the doorstep would be lost. Ecological politics only exists because independent parties have taken votes and worried even such hardline anti-environmentalists in the traditional parties as Mrs Thatcher. Greens have a dual function – by existing they put pressure on other parties and governments, while at the same time creating an alternative outside the conventional political status quo.

Environmental pressure groups within the traditional political parties have had a mixed history. SERA (Socialist Environment and Resources Association) and the Liberal Ecology Group have had limited success. SERA managed to turn around the Labour Party's pro-nuclear policies after working hard on the powerful TGWU. The Liberals accepted a commitment to zero economic growth and endorsed the conclusions of *Blueprint for Survival*, but such victories have been short lived, the new SLD is pro-growth and increasingly pro-nuclear re-armament. Neil Kinnock has crushed the left including the decentralized, greenish left associated with the GLC. Nuclear power and weapons are creeping back into the speeches and policy documents. In Germany the SPD, despite grassroots pressure, remains firmly pro-NATO and pro-nuclear. Activist pressure for disarmament was spectacularly ignored by the former Liberal leader David Steel. His successor Paddy Ashdown, an ex-SAS officer, shifted from unilateralism to keeping Trident. No conventional party looks likely to unambiguously reject nuclear weapons, criticize growth or decentralize power out of their own hands.

Such a leadership craves the support of Greens but is loath to take on board the ideas necessary to solve our present crisis. Neil Kinnock is a 'clientist' or exponent of a shopping list politics that seeks to add up the votes of women's groups, environmentalists, nurses, the homeless, etc., to make an electoral majority in return for key concessions.[4] As one member of the Fabians warned the environmental movement, 'The real tragedy would be if it ended as the Campaign for Nuclear Disarmament did, with prominent supporters quietly joining a new Labour government and swallowing the policies they had campaigned against, with none of the fundamental issues resolved.'[5] Co-option kills, but the threat is not just from Labour. Bill Rodgers, a viciously unecological transport minister and later an SDP MP, argued that fifty marginal constituencies could be won on the Green vote. As others have put it most bluntly, 'The Green issue will not go away. The correct and healthy Tory reaction is to expropriate it.'[6] The Greens must expropriate the expropriators.

Despite rapid growth it remains to be seen whether Green parties will be able to build a permanent basis of support. Many observers argue that as soon as Greens look like succeeding a cautious electorate will turn away from them. A party that promises fewer consumer goods and negative growth has, according to all conventional thinking, a bleak future. Yet if Greens gained no votes at all, electoral activity would still be of enormous value. The opportunity to talking to thousands of people through public debates, the media and canvassing is of great importance. If people are fundamentally to change their views, they will do so only after much discussion. If the population was already fully committed to Green politics, Green parties would hardly need to exist. As it is, without serious efforts to spread and deepen awareness the Green movement will be limited to the few and grow slowly if at all. Without the efforts of Green parties, Green politics will almost certainly be defined by the powers that be as superficial and swiftly co-optable environmentalism. There will always be Greens in traditional political parties (even if conservative ones), but their positions will be strengthened by external Green electoral activity.

Even the most traditional forms of conservation concern can lead to political awareness. Environmental concerns are high on the agenda: recent publicity has made virtually everyone aware of the problems of nuclear power, acid rain, the ozone layer and the greenhouse effect. We have seen how conventional politicians have responded to the greenhouse effect by promoting nuclear power as a viable alternative. Yet to reduce energy consumption goods will have to be made to last, the environment will have to come before money and decentralization will become a necessity. The Green movement thus has a whole series of opportunities to put environmental issues into a *political* context and push for fundamental change.

There is no reason why widespread concern cannot be turned into votes. The number of voters supporting radical change is growing. Green parties exist from Finland to British Columbia.[7] Even Brazil has a Green Party fighting to save the rainforests in alliance with a left-wing and increasingly successful Workers Party.[8] Greens have been elected to the highest levels of administration in many countries. Even in Britain the Party received 15% of the vote in the 1989 European Elections and came second in many constituencies.

The need to fight for a sustainable future and to define human worth other than in terms of £s or $s, is not a difficult message to understand nor one that can be seen as in the interest of just one class or group. Greens need to question their middle class roots and start working in a consistent and down-to-earth way. Green politics, despite the arguments of the Post-materialists,[9] should be made as material as possible; about food, work, health, the quality of life and most materially of all, about the very issue of survival. There is nothing intrinsically abstract or self-sacrificing about Green politics, if argued for and worked for seriously and practically. Global problems need to be put into a local context, with activists pointing to decaying tower blocks, congested roads and devastated monocultured landscapes. By putting forward practical solutions and getting involved in positive action as well as protest the constituency can be extended and long-term support built.

Using community politics, the Liberal Party increased its

number of councillors from 100 in 1962 to over 3,000 in the mid eighties.[10] Community politics should be pursued as an end rather than as a means of electing councillors. Green parties should organize around discrete areas and look at how they might 'green' their city, street or ward. Local action can be a way forward when wider change is blocked by conservative national governments. Community action can be used to make politics down-to-earth and accessible. 'Think globally, act locally' will need to become more than just a slogan.

Far from being a single-issue movement, activists should emphasize the holistic nature of their message. Left, Right and Centre politics have become almost exclusively the politics of money. Debate usually goes little further than exploring how much will be spent and by whom. Labour would invest more in the health service, Conservatives claim they are already spending enough and push for privatization. Greens go further and ask why people get ill in the first place, looking at the links between mind, body and society and pushing for more preventative medicine and funding for holistic alternatives. Pollution, poverty and the multinational drug companies all come under critical attention. On employment Greens argue that work needs to be personally satisfying and socially useful. Conventional parties seem to think any kind of work is sufficient.

Greens have to fight elections effectively. Good organization with plenty of election workers is obviously vital. Election material should put basic issues into a local context and into simple language. Eye catching posters are important. But above all canvassing, the act of going around talking to people, is essential. Canvassing can be used to generate ideas and to keep in touch with what people want as opposed to what a small clique of activists separate from the community would like to believe they want. It is also a way of starting dialogue at the grassroots. The most important reason why people don't support Green politics is because they have never met a Green candidate or activist. Canvassing a ward at every election over a period of four or five years almost always has good results.[11] It can be used not merely to target potential supporters but to challenge misconceptions and act as a catalyst for ecological action at a local level.

## The poverty of 'pragmatism'

But Green parties, even electorally successful ones, are no panacea. Greens like Jonathon Porritt and Sara Parkin are keen to label themselves as 'neither Left nor Right but ahead', rejecting the bureaucracy and compromise of conventional socialist parties. What they forget is that the same pressures that have corrupted such parties, who also originally aimed to emancipate humanity and to empower the powerless, will also threaten the Greens. To proclaim one's supposed radicalism is no defence against institutional pressures that propel one to conservativism and compromise. To paraphrase George Santana, those who do not learn from history, will be forced to repeat it.

The authors of one recent book on 'green politics' claim that 'Greens should have no reservations about the concept of leadership,'[12] and argue that while Green parties are an instrument with which to achieve a Green society, they should not behave in a specifically decentralized or Green fashion. Such an approach is frighteningly naïve and does nothing to prepare the Greens for the pressures that parliamentary institutions will put them under. In particular, Greens – especially in Britain and France – are ignorant of what has been termed 'the iron law of oligarchy', whereby political parties come to be dominated by a small number of officials who soon gain almost total control over the membership. Instead of working for change such cliques more often than not become obsessed with holding on to personal power and gaining positions of ever greater authority. Radical policies are rejected because compromise makes it easier to get into Parliament, while extra-parliamentary activity is viewed as a dangerous diversion. Michels in his *Political Parties* pointed out that all large organizations need full-time workers and that such workers all too easily develop into a 'political class' who, through access to the lines of comunication within a party plus the external media and with polished skills of speaking and writing, can maintain control and increasingly work not for the party or the interests of wider humanity but for themselves. Michels notes that any political leadership will tend to fossilize into a self-defensive clique:

> When faced with a threat to their authority or office from within the organization, the leaders will become extremely

> aggressive and will not hesitate to undermine many democratic rights. To lose command of their organization is to lose that which makes them important individuals, and hence they are strongly motivated to preserve their position even if it requires using repressive methods. They legitimize such behaviour by pointing out that a mass organization is inevitably an organization maintaining itself by its struggle with powerful and evil opponents. Therefore all efforts to introduce factionalism into the organization, to challenge the appropriateness of party or organization policy, result in aid and comfort to its enemies. Serious criticism of the leadership is thus defined as treachery to the organization itself.[13]

Such an approach usually leads to collusion with the forces earlier opposed, compromise with one's enemies to maintain influence over former 'friends' within the party. The classic example was the U-turn of the German Social Democratic Party on the eve of the First World War, who shifted from radical pacifism and a policy of general strike in the event of war, to support for the Kaiser and Prussian militarism. This change of heart was so stunning that even Lenin, a violent critic of the party, could not believe that it was possible for a party to change so quickly. He was convinced that the party newspaper's call for full support of the war effort was a forgery.

In our day the media will attack policies of fundamental importance such as decentralization, non-violence and opposition to accumulations of wealth and power as 'extreme' and electorally unpopular, trying to convince the Greens that they have either to change their policies or give up any hopes of influence within the system. After the 1989 European Elections the British press claimed that few Green voters knew of the party's opposition to economic growth and commitment to unilateralism, insisting that the Greens could not maintain electoral support with such dangerous ideas. Indeed the 1989 UK Green Party European Manifesto left out key areas of policy that were thought to be 'difficult to market' – like animal rights and much of the party's economic programme. Ultimately Green parties may reject Green politics and replace them with environmentalism, a hollow doctrine unable to get to the social and economic roots of environmental problems. Parliamentary compromise could be seen leading yet again to disillusionment amongst activists along with apathy and despair on the part of voters. The 'success' of Green parties at the expense of Green policies could become a way of damping down concern over the global crisis and allowing the destruction rooted in capitalism, patriarchy and global injustice to continue all the more ferociously. By compromising with the system the Green movement could well buy it just enough time to kill all of us and the planet. Greens cannot afford to have any illusions about the nature of political power and need to back up their activities with a sound understanding of the way the 'system' works.

It will be difficult but there are ways of breaking the 'iron law'. Green politics cannot be 'modernized' or sanitized to get votes through some form of 'new realism' (or other new ways of describing old-fashioned compromise). Radicals must go beyond Brian Gould's statement that 'Market research will tell us what the voters want, then it is up to us to provide the policies to match.' Green politics has to be about changing minds rather than going along with a pro-nuclear consensus and the pursuit of the yuppie vote. Ideas cannot be jettisoned for electoral success. What people think is power; debate is needed to bring about change. What is the point of being elected at the cost of one's politics? For example, Greens – in contrast to the British Labour Party – insist that far from being some kind of embarrassing social disease, unilateralism is vital to our very survival. Nuclear weapons demand the production of nuclear waste, so that without even a single button being pushed the 'deterrent' still sacrifices children and starves the poor of this planet. The risk of accident is infinitely higher than the risk of invasion. The links between the arms race and the profits and prestige of the arms manufacturers should be made clear. Alternative forms of defence that are cheaper, safer and more democratic should be promoted. It is not a question of ends and means. On defence, animal rights, agriculture and sexual politics, the dumping of key values to gain parliamentary seats is immoral was well as unrealistic.

Far from being 'pragmatic' so as to gain power (or more usually an illusion of power), Greens should use the strengths of the system they face and turn them around, rather than being turned themselves like radical movements in the past. In electoral systems without proportional representation 10% of the vote usually equals that margin between the two largest contending parties who will need to change radically if they are to gain the Green votes necessary to gain office. In systems with PR a similar sized Green vote would eventually give the Greens the ability to make or break governing coalitions and should also be exploited. There are levers that can be used within electoral systems without jettisoning the policies necessary to prevent global catastrophe.

## Holistic politics

A Green party (however non-oligarchical and non-conforming to the traditional model of party politics) has a limited role: change cannot be brought about purely through parliament. Greens need to work in a holistic way – promoting new ideas, building practical alternatives and *contesting elections*. By contesting and winning elections Greens will be able to put more energy from newly gained supporters into practical projects. As Green ideas spread, support for economic and practical alternatives will grow and encourage yet more people to vote for a real alternative to the politics of capitalism and growth. The snowball will have been set in motion and grow ever larger. Elections should not become a substitute for, but act as a catalyst towards, empowering people. It is dangerous to say 'Vote for us and we will Green the Earth'. This reinforces apathy. It is far more valuable to use elections as a way of talking to large numbers of people about the ecological crisis and encouraging them to take action. 'Vote Green but don't just vote . . .' is a useful way of promoting extra-parliamentary action via electoral politics. By challenging widely held illusions about the nature of power Greens may be able to resist the usual fate of radical parties in the past and be in a position to bring about change. It won't be easy though.

Greens should be as democratic as possible. Such minimum leadership as is necessary should act to dissolve itself; leading in the sense of allowing people to lead themselves (I have to admit that achieving this will be a first in political history!). Whatever the oligarchs and party officials say to justify their positions, it should be pointed out that the end of Green politics is a self-organizing, self-managed society, where human beings collectively decide their own fate, instead of being controlled by harsh economic processes or cold hierarchical structures. Self-organization is not just desirable but a vital prerequisite of a Green future. Ends do not justify means but are determined by them. As Dave Dellinger has put it, 'We had better aim not at seizing power but at eroding, undermining, democratizing, decentralizing and distributing.'[14]

To maintain support in the face of hostile press coverage and concerted pressure from the traditional parties, Greens should not compromise key values but instead concentrate on getting the message over at a grassroots level. Practical action will again be vital. Setting up networks for organic producers, creating ethical investment trusts or supporting city farms, will all help people to see that positive change is possible. Benefit gigs or concerts, picnics on threatened heath land or prehistoric sites might help knit activists together and make politics seem more worthwhile. Organic produce networks, mass bike rides or trespasses into bases or EEC grain silos can be used to make political activity more interesting and dynamic. Learning exchanges or co-operative bulk buying will make life easier for activists. Green Fairs and events can be used to link diverse but potentially allied groups. Greens need to transform communities in whatever way possible and promote personal and collective action.

Pressure from below will be vital if elected representatives are to stay Green. Green councillors will need supporting as well as guarding or else they will become stale and stressed. Activists will need plenty of help to overcome the often corrupting and certainly exhausting ways of local councils, national parliaments and senates. Rotation has had a very mixed history but it is surely bad for Green politics and bad for the individuals involved to sit as councillors or members of parliament for too long. The Green and Radical Alternative European Link (GRAEL), the very successful group of Green, socialist and regionalist members of the European Parliament, has at least partially overcome the problem by giving every MEP (the knight) a helper (the squire) who learns how the system works while giving support. Eventually the roles are reversed and the helper takes his or her place as an MEP. Such a system is far from perfect (a less sexist way of describing it to visitors to the European Parliament would be valuable) but it is progress in the right direction. It is not a matter of rejecting all organization because hierarchies are evil, or accepting hierarchy because it is efficient (it isn't), but of finding specifically Green ways of organizing. Decentralization is vital, top-heavy organizations are easily toppled, tough and meshed grassroots are more difficult to dig out.

## Conservatism and cybernetics

But even strong roots that are allowed to grow over decades are no guarantee of success. Fundamental change will be difficult to achieve, even if the oligarchs can be fought off. History is littered with the graves of proto-green organization. What did the Diggers or the Levellers, the Utopian Socialists, the Chartists or even the nineteenth-century co-operative movement achieve? What happened to Gandhi's heirs? Co-opt or die is the rule. The Russian communists and Western social democrats are the exceptions that prove the rule. The Green movement has not yet been able to introduce a fundamental change, and radical policies have been contained within a conservative system; Green political strategy remains ill thought-out and ineffectual in real terms.

Such a failure has been made most clear in Germany. The fundamentalists, who argue that the Greens must remain an anti-party party and cannot in any circumstances support the Social Democrats, are left outside the system, consigned to impotency. The realos, by allying with the Social Democrats to keep out the Christian Democrats, have no way of preserving their politics from the reformism that corroded the socialism of the SPD. Already noted realos have argued that the Greens should reject controversial policies, notably their opposition to NATO, and get into government. Either way Greens will achieve little or nothing and, through their arguments and inaction, alienate popular support.

In a far from unhealthy way all human beings tend to be conservative. Sudden and drastic change is unsettling. Political activity involves sacrifice and disruption in both social and political terms but without such political change the consequences in terms of ecological damage, flooding, mass poverty and eventual mass destruction will be far more radical. We are also enmeshed in a political system that values and seeks to preserve hierarchical advantage and accumulated wealth. But at a deeper level we must understand that systems tend to conserve their basic structures.

In political terms, reform to retain the nature of the system is the rule. The growth of Green politics has been met by the superficial but highly visible greening of the old-fashioned parties, so as to undercut the electoral basis of the new force. The most obvious forms of pollution and environmental damage are cleaned up, so as to allow pollution and environmental destruction to continue. The dirtiest factory in Britain manufactures smokeless fuel.[15] Minor reform is used to block major change. So far Green politics has aimed at reform, arguing that ever increasing legislation is needed to restrict pollution and encourage conservation. The contradiction between the need for new nationally imposed laws and decentralization is obvious. What is less obvious but even more important is the effect such reforms will have on the possibilities of real change. Reforms whether from traditional parties or future Green governments tend to have the effect of hiding or removing the most obvious forms of damage, without tackling the roots of crisis. A little action or even quite a lot may be worse than none at all.

For example, the test ban treaty (which stopped the suicidal atmospheric testing of nuclear weapons) helped to reduce public concern; it led directly to the decline of CND and helped to strengthen the arms race. As we saw earlier, the Labour Party helped the process along. Ironically, the current START agreement will remove land based missiles from public view and put them on the sea, where the risk of catastrophe is greater. The test ban treaty was vital, just as today it is vital that alternatives to CFC aerosols are developed. We need to clean up the North Sea, but we have to understand and immobilize the basic motor of destruction as well as cleaning the wounds and treating the symptoms.

Reform won't work, but revolutionary change is not an alternative, at least not in the conventional Marxist/Leninist sense. Things need to grow rather than be forced through the dialectics of violence. Revolutions often end by incorporating the worst aspects of the regimes they overthrow. The formula of 'Thesis (Capitalists) + Anti-Thesis (Working Class) = Synthesis (Socialism)' is political arithmetic that no longer adds up.

We need to find some way of swinging society into another mode, where it will naturally defend itself against attempts to reintroduce capitalist growth, hierarchy and ecological destruction. Neither paper mountains (recycled or otherwise) of parliamentary legislation, nor violent upheaval, will bring about an ecological society. Greens need to pioneer a non-violent revolution based upon a new political model. Both Marxism and Liberalism, as theories of political action developed in the last century, have lost their force, Greens need a new guide to action.

One that may fill the gap can be developed from systems theory or cybernetics. Cybernetics describes systems that tend towards stability and resist change. Political, economic and social sub-systems can be modelled in such a way. Greens are not just up against capitalism and power structures or greedy individuals or perhaps 'human nature', but the conservatism of system dynamics as well.

External change (the growth of the Green movement) tends to be met by compensating internal change (reform) aimed at maintaining the basic integrity of the system – a process of *negative* feedback. Internal movement cancels out external shifts. A good example of feedback in a system comes from the human body. As the temperature increases (external change) we naturally start to sweat (internal change), so as to compensate for hotter conditions and cool down (negative feedback). Incremental change proposed by 'liberal pragmatists' in the form of new laws and reforms will simply strengthen the system without changing its real nature.

There is an alternative. Some forms of change can lead to chain reactions that change the nature of a system, whether political, social or biological. Greens must try to create such *positive* feedback, which causes the system to add to, rather than compensate for, external pressure. Instead of perspiring, positive feedback would makes us get even hotter and hotter until our physical nature changed in a quite dramatic way. Instead of engineering revolution, pushing for reformism or writing blueprints, Greens should push for change that induces further change and leads to a different system.

For example, by introducing subsidies for low input agriculture and removing them from energy intensive crops, the demand for organic produce would grow fast. Land holdings would become smaller and would need to be worked more labour intensively. Rural communities would revive. Wildlife would flourish. Things would move forward far more effectively from one well thought-out piece of legislation than from a dozen byzantine plans. Greens need to be able to distil such pieces of transitional legislation into a few key ideas that would look relatively harmless to other political groups, be obviously popular with voters and lead to widespread change. Easier said than done, but at least more productive than negative reform or conservative revolutionary posturing.

Changes should be thought out in terms of the maximum effect in an ecological direction and their importance to people's daily lives, belief systems and economic structures. Ironically Thatcherism is an example albeit in the wrong direction. The Conservative government's sale of council houses and shares reinforced support for the Conservatives and capitalism, allowing it to bring in even more right-wing legislation. Poll tax has discouraged many anti-conservative voters from placing themselves on the electoral register.[16] High unemployment has weakened trade unions and helped to lower wages, concentrating power even more. Legislation reinforces social trends that strengthen the government's ability to create further legislation. Greens should build rather than destroy, redistributing power and wealth in the opposite direction.

Closely akin to such a holistic model of political practice is the idea of acting as a catalyst rather than a vanguard. Greens must organize just as effectively and seriously as any other party but take on a much wider role. Winning elections can only be part of a much wider strategy of accelerating positive humane and ecological change. Local Green parties and groups should set up skills exchanges so that members and activists can learn how to lobby councillors, speak publicly, design leaflets, build dry stone walls or make videos. Chaos is hardly empowering and it is unrealistic to assume that everybody can do everything. But individuals should have the opportunity to learn. Structures should be as open as possible; obviously posts and tasks should be rotated whenever possible to take pressure off individuals, to spread experience and inhibit the growth of hierarchy. Politics should be about getting people involved: everyone should have something to do however small. Virtually everybody has some kind of skill or the ability to learn how to do something. A poster designed, a street canvassed or a demonstration organized will encourage further activity. People need to be gently involved and then they can draw others in.

Green politics will only be effective if Green groups and parties work in every corner of the globe seeking local change in the context of international problems. National and international groups should seek to bring Greens together when a common approach is needed to tackle larger institutions such as the parliaments, the EEC or World Bank. Greens internationally as well as locally should work to encourage organization instead of imposing it.

Getting the theory right won't be enough. The practicalities of Green politics will be equally difficult. Even vital change will be challenged by vested interests. From phone tapping to media smears to the government executioner portrayed in the BBC play *Edge of Darkness*, the state has many tools at its disposal.[17] However strongly the alternative grows, the backlash will grow faster. According to Gandhi, 'Every good movement passes through five stages; indifference, ridicule, abuse, repression and respect . . .'[18] Perhaps respect is the most dangerous stage of all. Co-option or extermination comes afterwards. The multinationals will spot the challenge and act against it, before it knows its own nature.

Green politics, which is already growing fast, will eventually collide with what Marx termed 'the most violent, mean and malignant passions of the human breast, the Furies of private interest'.[19] To resist such monsters the Green movement will need to develop workable economic alternatives and beware blistering attacks. Green politics *is* possible; Green economics will be very much more difficult.

# 5
# Economics

Building an entirely new kind of economic system that meets human needs within ecological constraints won't be easy. To sustain itself a sustainable economic system will have to erode capitalism and provide a workable alternative, which would distribute goods and services without traditional centralized planning or market mechanisms: the former being too inefficient and the latter tending towards capital concentration and economic growth.

## The first day in office

A Green government will be controlled by the economy rather than being in control. On coming to office through coalition or more absolute electoral success, it would be met by an instant collapse of sterling as 'hot money' and entrepreneurial capital went elsewhere. The exchange rate would fall and industrialists would move their factories to countries with more relaxed environmental controls and workplace regulation. Sources of finance would dry up as unemployment rocketed, slashing the revenue from taxation and pushing up the social security bills. The money for ecological reconstruction – the building of railways, the closing of motorways and construction of a proper sewage system – would run out. The International Monetary Fund is notoriously allergic to providing loans to finance negative growth. The parliamentary levers of power don't reach very far. Mrs Thatcher only survived economic recession with the full support of Fleet Street, the City, and big business – unlikely allies for even the most respectable Green administration.

## Economic contradictions

Even if given a fair chance Green economic policy would run into major problems. Resource, energy and pollution taxes, as well as being regressive, would play a highly contradictory role. If they succeed in their objectives of reducing pollution and cutting energy and resource waste, such taxes will clearly fail as a long-term source of revenue. They will only raise revenue on a sustainable basis in a society that continues to waste energy and cause environmental damage. Pollution needs to be stopped, not taxed!

The basic income scheme works or doesn't work in just the same way. By paying everybody a basic income whether they work or not, it aims to reduce formal paid forms of work, to encourage community activity and to give people enough economic security to escape the rat race. But without a steady source of income from the rates it would soon become unworkable. On the other hand, if enough people continued to work in the formal economy, its original intentions would have surely failed. As a transitional strategy it might just work, if income tax revenues fell at the same rate that local currencied or non-monetary economies became strong enough to survive without external help, but it would be a gamble.

It is very difficult to see how Green economics could function in theory or practice. It is not enough to point out the weaknesses of conventional economics and criticize indicators like GNP without producing an alternative economic model. A Green economy would be built on assumptions so different from our present one that it is difficult to see how the transition could be made smoothly, if at all. Green economics is about minimizing material consumption, energy usage, formal work and monetary flows. Conventional economics in all its variants is about the opposite; maximizing consumption and growth. Within a modern economy, as we have seen, minimizing consumption would lead to chaos, although increasing it or even keeping it at present levels would lead to biological collapse.

Neither workers' control nor the growth of community business outlined by Guy Dauncey and others would solve the growth problem.[1] Neither the idealized 'workers' nor the 'small businessmen' would have an incentive to go for negative or zero growth.[2] Technically it may be possible to produce light bulbs that last virtually for ever, but the workers co-operative that made such light bulbs would go out of business. No car manufacturer would fund research into the permanent car. The demand for goods would slump, pollution and waste would be cut, energy consumption would fall, individuals wouldn't have to earn so much money to replace cars and light bulbs unless they really wanted to. Prosperity and ecology could be united but none of this would help destitute Ford workers or the owners of community light fitting shops.

Even if the light bulb dilemma could be overcome, distribution would be problematic. Free market economies governed by the price mechanism tend to lead to ever greater capital concentration as individual small firms invest, gain from the economies of scale and squeeze the market of many into the oligopoly of a few. There is plenty of evidence to suggest that however small business structures start out, the logic of profit and capital leads to growth and concentration. The market is oiled by money which acts as a signal and an incentive for firms to produce more of a good when shortages push up price. Money communicates the demand of some consumers smoothly to producers but ignores the demands of those without money in the market place, future generations, the poor, and other species. Monetary rewards encourage firms to manipulate and increase demand through advertizing, built-in obsolescence and other Machiavellian techniques of persuasion. Supply and demand eat up today, without a thought, the natural resources that should be discounted for tomorrow. 'Shortage causes higher prices, which stimulate further efforts to catch fish, which makes the shortage worse, and so on, until there are no fish.'[3] Once again it has to be repeated: *Ecology is incompatible with the market.*

But would the usual posited alternative of socialist planning work? From what we have seen of Chinese deforestation, Polish pollution and Soviet nuclear disasters, one would suspect not. It has to be admitted that so far planned economies have been governed by market pressure and have copied some of the worst features of the market, particularly the religious concepts of unrestrained technological 'advance', giantism and 'progress'. The USSR and China need to earn hard currency through exports. In the same way as individual firms compete and through competition attempt to gain market dominance, East and West have competed. State socialism trying to prove its worth by outgrowing the West has turned into mirror-image state capitalism. From the early days of the Soviet Union through to America's contra war with Nicaragua, capitalist countries have tried to disrupt economies through war, trade sanctions and refusal of aid. But even without such pressure it is difficult to see how they could act effectively or ecologically. Environmental problems have already been discussed but the inefficiency of traditional socialist planning is another issue. 'Mathematicians have calculated that in order to draft an accurate and fully integrated plan for material supply for the Ukraine for one year requires the labour of the entire population for 10 million years.'[4] You cannot calculate varied human wants with a large computer in a small room in the Kremlin – large scale planning does not work.

Frankel has put forward an interesting model of an eco-socialist economy combining some national and regional planning with co-operatives and some individuals working within a market sector, plus the idea of local production for local use by the mass of the population.[5] Such a model does take us closer to a Green economy, but even if the scenario is of a fully functioning economy that makes planning democratic and efficient or prevents the market from robbing both the poor and the planet, it still begs the question of how to get there. The real problem is how to break with the basic economic model of capitalism that demands continual economic growth just to stay in the same place. Frankel, alas, fails to come up with a strong mechanism for making the transition to eco-socialism. A Green economy will need to overcome the pressures of vested interests and structural inertia. Economic change will need to be introduced not through sudden revolution nor through swiftly put-together parliamentary legislation but evolution; slowly, gradually and experimentally, starting from now rather than after the seizure of the Winter Palace or the Green landslide of 2022.

## How to smash capitalism gently

### *1: Consumer pressure*

Reduced consumption will be key to promoting ecological economics, reducing the power of large corporations and insulating local or national economies from external pressures. Yet as we have already stressed economic campaigns have to mean much more than hairshirtism and isolated individualistic action. We need collective support – for those who live in rural communities and still depend on cars, or communities served by only substandard shops selling junk food. Economic action is about weakening multinationals instead of blaming their victims. This said we should pause before buying anything. There are thousands of goods that are either unnecessary or could be borrowed, rented or shared instead of bought. The most subversive act in a consumer society is the refusal to consume; it is also one of the safest. 'The fact that General Motors may have a larger intelligence organization than Australia will yield it no power when most of us cycle or walk to work and choose to stay at home on our holidays.'[6]

Lifestyle commitment needs to be about consuming less, not just consuming differently. Instead of looking for CFC-free aerosols, we need to abandon aerosols altogether. We can live without air fresheners and hair sprays but we cannot live without the ozone layer. This said, selective boycotts may be necessary to buy time for the ozone layer and the rainforests while wider non-consumption has time to build up. We should reduce our consumption of cash crops but we should also buy cash crops from Traidcraft and other groups who pay a fair price to 'Third World' producers. We need to be gentle in our non-consumption. We should shift to a diet which is increasingly vegan and based on local organic produce, but this won't be easy for everybody. There need to be pit stops on the way – conservation grade cereals which are still produced with some pesticides and fertilizers, humanely produced meat rather than no meat at all, shop bought as opposed to allotment grown vegetables: getting there is a process, not a single event. Slater argues that to avoid money-think and over-consumption, we should seek to minimize our dependency on large impersonal bureaucracies, buy things only if we really need them and never own what we rarely use.[7] Such campaigns should not ignore politics. The kind of transitional measures discussed in the last chapter should include support for organic producers, better food labelling, encouragement to smallholders and other ways of making reduced consumption easier. Economic campaigns are vital: in a market system money talks louder than legislation or lobbying.

Such campaigns can go beyond simple boycotts. The Animal Liberation Front did millions of pounds of damage to factory farms and vivisection laboratories in the 1970s and 1980s, raising the profile of what had been only a tiny movement and at the same time making animal abuse too expensive for many firms. One measure of the ALF's success has been the amount of state repression directed at its activists through the courts, Fleet Street and the Special Branch at a time when the powers that be have ignored openly revolutionary organizations like the Socialist Workers Party and Workers Revolutionary Party.[8,9] But the backlash that put Ronnie Lee, the ALF's founder by then retired from active service, in jail for ten years has led to a serious shift from his policy of 'economic violence' with increasing frustration leading to fire bombing and risk to human life.

### *2: Imploding capitalism*

At the opposite end of the spectrum is John Elkington's concept of 'Green Capitalism', which has had a very different reception from the media and traditional politicians.[10] In essence it argues that growth is permissible and market problems can be solved by market pressure. Ecology can be consumed and commodified like anything else in our economy. 'Green Capitalism' is reformist, making minor change to sustain an unsustainable system, but despite all this it has the potential to subvert the business interests it seeks to defend. Anita Roddick is at least partly motivated by profit, and even if she wasn't, the shareholders of her franchise chain (The Body Shop) certainly would be. Yet what is interesting is that through the increased growth of The Body Shop the profits of companies like ICI are reduced by the replacement of chemicals with natural products. Wholefood stores reduce the profits of the traditional food corporations who add value in the form of cheap bulk – increasing fat and sugar – and sell bran taken from white bread to agribusiness.

Holistic preventative medicine will slow the growth of pharmaceutical consumption. Expansive, accelerating capitalism can be made to implode through its own dynamics; the growth of some businesses will reduce overall growth and destruction. The imploding capitalist would overcome the 'light bulb' dilemma by producing light bulbs that lasted for ever, massively reducing light bulb consumption, putting himself or herself temporarily out of business before looking for new areas of economic implosion such as the everlasting fridge or toaster.

One danger is that Green capitalism will go in for explosive activity using environmental destruction to create more growth. Replacing formerly free or very cheap 'goods' like clean air and water with the need for filters and masks will boost profits and minimize pressure for change by cocooning individuals against the effects of pollution. There already exists 'a whole industrial complex for manufacturing and installing pollution control systems, made up essentially of those firms whose activity is at the source of the worst pollution!'[11] Health foods, especially vitamin pills and other supplements, allow firms like Holland and Barrett (at the time of writing owned by sugar producers Tate and Lyle) a new means of generating profit and largely unnecessary waste through 'alternative' concerns.

Another risk is that individual actions will be used to justify corporate and institutional inaction. Economic change, to be effective, demands collective co-operation and structural change. Buying organic produce is difficult, but buying it collectively is a lot better. The transition to a Green economy will only come about if people get together and work co-operatively to change things. Individual change as we have already noted is not enough.

### *3: Alternative investment*

Investment also has interesting potential. It can be used to subvert the market by putting ethics and sustainability before profit, so as to stand Adam Smith's approach to the market on its head. Through mortgages, pension funds, insurance schemes, local authority and personal investment, we all directly or indirectly have economic power. Many of the major US and UK banks have directly funded rainforest destruction in South America. Little in the way of Building Society money goes into well-insulated, ecological housing. Animal charities have investments in companies that use vivisection or promote factory farming. Trade unions paradoxically invest pension funds in capitalist enterprises that justify low wages and poor working conditions in terms of profit for shareholders.

Such self-exploitation has to be stopped. At present virtually all our monies are being used to fund growth and destruction. We need to pull our money out of conventional institutions and start funding alternatives. In 1988 £144 million was invested 'ethically' in Britain and at least 10% of the money on Wall Street now has some kind of ethical tie, but such sums remain tiny in comparison to the bulk of *un*ethical funds. In any case, rather than being invested in what is positive, such funds avoid just a few of the worst negatives; corporate involvement in South Africa, tobacco, arms and alcohol. Less than 1% of 'ethical' investment is put into ecological projects: 99% of it is invested to create growth. Ethical investment can be seen as a way of window-dressing the whole process of consumer-capitalist destruction in a typically reformist way; combining ethics and the market rather than challenging the system fundamentally. What it does do is to show that profit is not the only or even the main criterion for making economic decisions. This fact alone makes ethical investment a profoundly subversive notion.

Green investment would go beyond existing ethical investment by deliberately taking funds away from the present system and using them to promote specifically ecological production. It is not enough to invest in pollution control equipment; profits would grow only with increasing environmental destruction. No pollution would equal no end-of-year dividend and a declining portfolio. The Ecology Building Society which invests in specifically ecological housing is already thriving in Britain. Mercury Provident have developed a banking institution based on the principles of Rudolf Steiner, where investors can choose rates of return and the type of project they want to support. In Germany Die Grünen have recycled their massive state funds into women's refuges, cinemas, alternative energy parks and hundreds of other projects through the Öko-fund. An important transitional demand would be to make ecological investment easier and allow for the creation of local community banks. Green economic change does not have to wait for institutional change – we all have the opportunity to make our money work for sustainability instead of destruction, so we should start using it.

### *4: Workers' power*

The labour movement has often acquiesced with the bosses rather than campaign for ecological protection. Unions like the electricians' EEPTU and the engineers' AUEW have strongly supported nuclear power, while the TUC opposed the European Community's 1983 directive aimed at restricting titanium dioxide pollution of the North Sea because of the effect on jobs. But those of us who work in the formal sense have the power to withdraw our labour and to campaign for change at the point of production. Trade unions have long been involved in Green bans in Australia, and in the UK the National Union of Seamen have blocked the sea dumping of nuclear waste. The trade union movement, currently under siege, has much to gain from moving from a sectional interest to the wider defence of community interests which would give them popular support difficult for right wing politicians and corporate union busters to dislodge. Trade union environmentalism is based on the fact that pollution often hurts workers before harming the wider environment and that by campaigning for health and safety at work, unions fight for all of us. Factory farming is not only cruel but creates dust and disease that harms workers. The fire brigade union has opposed the building of a new nuclear power station at Hinkley Point on the grounds of safety and the problems their members would have in the event of a Chernobyl type accident where the initial fire fighters would inevitably sacrifice their lives. Capitalism cannot function without investment, raw materials and end consumers, nor can it function without labour – and workers have the potential to withdraw their labour so as to prevent the production of ecologically and socially damaging products. At present such actions would be political and thus 'illegal' under British anti-union legislation but the 1989 London Underground strikes have shown that unofficial union action from the grassroots can avoid the seizure of union funds and the punishment of officials. This said, unions should experiment with more creative (and no doubt illegal) forms of militancy; a bus strike hurts the disabled and the pensioner, a refusal on the part of the driver to accept fares, allowing people to travel free doesn't! Trade unions committed to self-management should answer the 'jobs versus environment' question by demanding shorter hours, production for use rather than profit, by arguing for worker and community control of co-operative enterprises.

The 'light bulb' dilemma might be resolved through variations of the Lucas plan, where it was proposed to produce socially useful items instead of military hardware. Even in a Green economy we would still need new goods, maintain old ones and generate standardized spare parts. The recycling industry would also boom. The trick would be to gradually reduce the workload, so as to avoid shock unemployment, whilst sharing out fairly the fruits of labour and the hours of production. The labour movement is not Green yet – often pollution, animal abuse and military production are still justified because they create jobs, concerns over pay still come before less co-optable demands for workers' control, the trade unions have often dismissed environmentalism and feminism as middle class luxuries – but it could be won over.

## *5: Commodity prices*

Another pillar of our present unsustainable system is the supply of cheap raw materials from the underdeveloped to the overdeveloped worlds. The North, insisting that export-led growth is the way forward, encourages the over-production of both cash crops and raw materials. But as the supply of such commodities increases, prices are pushed down and the terms of trade fall. To maintain income 'Third World' countries have to increase exports. It becomes even more difficult to raise export revenue, so the pressure to export more increases, further depressing prices. Land is taken from peasants to provide cash crops, soil erosion increases and natural resources are plundered to provide short term economic stability. We complain of the ignorance of Brazilians and Malaysians when they cut down trees but forget that our demand for the mineral resources beneath the forests propel the cycle of destruction.

A Green approach would conserve resources and restrict supply, so as to increase prices and narrow the gap between North and South. It would have an obvious attraction to countries in the 'Third World': in the 1970s the oil-producing countries showed that it was possible to increase revenue by reducing the supply of oil, shifting the terms of trade on to a fairer basis and giving the 'First World' a strong material incentive to cut growth and promote conservation. Similar cartels could be constructed for other mineral resources, protecting ecologically important areas, at least in the short term, while promoting the pressures necessary for their long term conservation.

It may be little more than a dream. The North will hardly look on quietly as its economic power is eroded, but campaigners on the part of the peace and development movements in the North of the globe might help to minimize military or economic intervention. Already the USA and USSR are finding it increasingly expensive and dangerous to intervene abroad. To get diverse countries in different parts of the globe and with varied political systems to act in unison will be more difficult.

Land reform will be vital if real development is to occur and trade advantages are not to be absorbed by national (as opposed to international) elites. Cash crops would have to be cut back and the urban bias of countries like Brazil and Kenya changed to emphasize rural development. Peasants could feed themselves, grow fuel crops on a sustainable basis and sell surpluses if they so wished – instead of growing cash crops while their children starved. A combination of agricultural self-sufficiency and local production for local need plus fair trade between 'Third World' countries (as opposed to unfair trade with the 'First World') would gain the support of many citizens south of the equator. The Green revolution of the 1990s might take on a very different meaning from that of the 1970s.

### *6: Building the alternative*

Political change cannot come from the peasants alone! So, having rejected Lenin, we should beware of embracing Mao. Greens need to build as well as erode and oppose. Widespread support for Green ideas will be difficult to win and sustain unless individuals can see Green alternatives working in practice. Islands of Green in an ocean of capitalism will be difficult to sustain. The failure of the GLC under the onslaught of Thatcherism shows that grassroots ecological activity cannot afford to rely on the local or national state. Sustainability cannot be funded on student grants (let alone loans) or unemployment benefit. Art centres, recycling schemes and city farms should not depend on the whims of central government or the wishes of right-wing councillors. Economic alternatives need to become free standing; self-sufficiency is a Green economic virtue.

Such a strategy sounds tough; it need not be. Greens should put their money and muscle into practical alternatives outside the state sector and narrowly commercial activities. The alternative will have to start now with people sharing resources, land and skills. Such efforts will feed back into a larger social base for Green activities, while at the same time creating the embryo of a different kind of economy. Large islands of co-operation, if not continents, can be built in the capitalist ocean. Picnics and parties, collective allotments, co-operative buying, shared meals, local community news sheets, learning exchanges, tithing, ecological transport . . . we can all, whatever our own circumstances, start somewhere and move forward into more serious economic activity. Local economic cycles with their own dynamic can be created.

One tool is to be found in the idea of the Local Employment and Trade Systems (LETS); essentially local currencies that encourage such collective activity and economic self-sufficiency. Individuals pay each other for services and goods in 'Green pounds' rather than with conventional money. There is no interest and accumulation is difficult, so such systems tend to smooth out inequalities while allowing for the regeneration of the most impoverished of local economies. Although operating successfully in numerous locations across the world such local currencies are illegal in Britain. Yet if introduced on a large enough scale and combined with community banking and increased self-sufficiency they would provide a way of overcoming the problems of national capital outflows, falling exchange rates and balance of payment difficulties.[12]

## A local economic system

As capitalism weakens and the alternative grows, groups will gain the strength necessary to create a sustainable economy in both the material and the biological senses; investing in local resource centres, sharing community capital such as road vehicles, word processors, knitting machines, welding equipment and bike tools, and producing autonomously. Libraries would be expanded and school facilities opened up to the whole population out of teaching hours. Many goods including some food items and simple clothing will be made, bartered or gift exchanged with neighbours on a local non-market basis. The domestic gift economy whereby people swap and share will complement the work of local institutions like libraries, community centres and colleges; together they will take on an important role in establishing a *local* economy.

## *The place of planning*

Monetary trade between regions and former nations would still of course be vital, although on a much reduced scale, but it would have to be fair trade. In the 1940s Professor Ragnar Frisch won a Nobel prize for producing a model of stable world trade whereby countries drew up lists of import and export items along with expected annual volume growth; prices could then be negotiated and mistakes paid or compensated for. Such a mechanism could be a way of encouraging fair and non-oppressive world planning for conservation and development. Planning by multinationals and Western governments already works on a global scale but in a less benevolent way.[13]

Within regional economies the communes imagined by Bahro and Gorz would have a role in producing more sophisticated goods such as the initial capital items needed for local production.[14] A measure of local planning on a decentralized basis involving elected representatives of consumers and producers would be vital. Some decisions would have to be taken on a regional or national level particularly in the allocation of raw materials. Even larger bodies would have some role in managing transport and telecommunications.

## *Redefining women's oppression?*

At present 'women's' work in the domestic economy is ignored by statisticians and seen as something that should be free, while 'productive' work is still used to define traditional male roles. High entropy tasks like cooking, cleaning or washing clothes which are unending, repetitive and largely unrewarded have a far lower status than tasks defined as 'work' that produce a measurable, concrete end item. Destroying the domestic sexual division of labour will be far from easy; the danger is that men will merely redefine some forms of domestic work as productive and worthy of rewarding while consigning women to new ghettos. Already where men cook and bring up children their efforts are hailed as revolutionary and almost heroic, while the daily domestic struggles of a million housewives receive far less attention than the activity of a handful of male equivalents. The feminization of a Green economy will demand more than the occasional bout of guilt-inspired washing up. Not only will stereotyped notions of male and female work have to go but there will have to be major efforts to end the divisions between manual (low status and far more a feature of women's lives than of men's 'work') and mental work, high entropy (low status) and 'productive' tasks as well as between work and leisure (looking after the kids?). All of this will demand a cultural revolution that will make Mao's effort to re-educate urban intellectuals on the land look somewhat puny. We would expect such a cultural revolution to be met by a hostile reaction from most men and some women, making a feminization process of this kind sound impossible; but combining domestic chores with what has been seen as traditional nine-to-five work would be one way of making *both* patterns of behaviour more attractive. Who after all wants to look after children all the time or work on the factory floor virtually every day of their life? Combining the two would make both better as long as women were not forced by a continuing male-dominated society into doing the least rewarding and lowest status tasks in both spheres.

So-called 'post-Fordist' work structures that employ individuals on a decentralized and part-time basis should not be mistaken for eco-feminism; franchises exploit workers (especially women) just as much as traditional forms of workplace organization if not more, but by giving the illusion of Greener employment they present a greater danger.

## *Wealth and redistribution*

Money in the usual sense would come to have a much reduced role. At present banks can expand the money supply almost infinitely through lending and the creation of credit; in essence bankers lend out eight or nine times the money they have deposited with them and reap a fortune back in interest. Bankers create money out of thin air. Modern banking demands continuous economic growth and without it banks would eventually collapse as creditors became impoverished. In a Green economy, no one would have the right to increase the money supply for private or corporate profit. Local community banks might be able to create a limited quantity of credit that might be lent to local projects after popular consultation.

Basic economic security demands that everyone is well housed. Second and third homes bought purely for investment purposes would be strongly discouraged. Legislation that encouraged sharing and a programme of house building and repair would all be important. If everyone had somewhere to live as a right, the need to buy homes and obtain a mortgage to do so would diminish sharply. In turn much of the pressure to work in the formal economy and to earn a regular, large income would be diminished.

Redistribution is difficult to achieve. Despite decades of progressive taxation intended to bring about a fairer spread of wealth and income, there are marked and growing disparities in Britain. The richest Americans each control a sum of wealth equal to the annual wage of 100,000 skilled workers.[15] In the UK 70% of land is held by just 1% of the population.[16] A restoration of common land stolen during the enclosures of the eighteenth century, along with an effective and sharply progressive land tax, would help redistribute what would be one of the main sources of wealth in a post-industrial society. The creation of a guaranteed income scheme via a unified taxation/benefits scheme would also help. It would be especially valuable if it incorporated a high threshold before income were taxed, along with steep marginal rates for the richest. If everyone had access to land, housing, a basic income and some form of productive capital, one of the major pressures for growth might be banished.

While taxes would be largely levied, spent and administered on a district or even ward level, there would need to be regional and national tiers to redistribute wealth from relatively prosperous to poorer areas – as happens to an extent even now. There would be little sense in allowing Britain's poorest borough of Hackney to go independent, although the north of England with plenty of land and houses might do better than the present

City of London after the decline of the money and capital markets.

Redistribution might be reinforced without discouraging energy saving through a sliding scale of charges with consumers paying more per unit as they consumed greater quantities of petrol or electricity. The usual 'unitax' alternative of a flat rate tax would keep the poor on the poverty line, cancelling the positive effects of a guaranteed income, increasing death among the elderly through hypothermia and doing little to stimulate the conservation efforts of those on high incomes who use the most energy.

A Basic Income Scheme might be made to succeed if, as Percival and Paul Goodman have suggested, guaranteed income was linked to a contribution of labour to the community on a part-time basis. Basic income would certainly stand a much greater chance of succeeding if funded partly through LETS, instead of depending upon but at the same time progressively undermining the formal economic sector of conventionally paid work.

## A post socialist / post capitalist economy

Ultimately things would have to go beyond fiscal change however imaginative. An ecological economy would need to become more than a state-funded by-product of the capitalist market. A Green economy would have to maintain its own equilibrium without constant prodding from bureaucrats, however ecological. It is easier to see what is wrong with the old models than to create a new economic cycle. In the same way it would have been difficult for medieval people to have predicted industrialism or for communities that operated with barter to understand the concept of money: we will have to make a qualitative mental jump if we are to understand how a future post-capitalist, post-socialist economy will function.

The key to all economics is human motivation. As the editor remarked on reading the first draft of this chapter, rented and shared items actually need replacing faster than privately owned goods because people in our present society do not look after them as well as goods they feel they 'own'. In self-managed Yugoslavia workers in the vine growing areas and hop fields had Mercedes in the garages, while those in other self-managed sectors were forced to migrate to escape their poverty. Even a co-operatively managed LET system would not on its own guarantee economic stability or even relative equality; those with the most skills – doctors, plumbers and teachers – would force the rest of humanity into the 'dirty' tasks and cause the system to stagnate as they acquired more and more of the 'Green dollars'. It would be nice to see a non-animal-abusing version of Marx's famous dictum that one 'will hunt in the morning, fish in the afternoon, rear cattle in the evening and be a literary critic after dinner, without ever becoming a hunter, a fisherman, a herdsmen or critic.' We need help to overcome such skill-based inequalities and allow all of us, for our own benefit and that of society as a whole, to combine both manual and mental work. Nove cynically rewrites the above, 'Men [sic] will freely decide to repair aero-engines in the morning, fill teeth in the early afternoon, drive a heavy lorry in the early evening, without being an aero-engine maintenance artificer, dentist, lorry-driver, or cook,' to show how far we are from such a vision.[17] Certainly a Green economy for totally pragmatic reasons will have to be a more altruistic one than we have at present; as Auden noted in a different context, we must love each other or die. In short, an ecological economy will demand internal as well as external change.

Adam Smith's model of the free market worked (at least in a limited sense) by meeting material needs. But such material 'needs' over and above the basics of food, clothing and shelter are cultural; we don't need televisions in an intrinsic sense. The Vikings did not suffer in any particular way because they lacked compact disc players. High resolution television will one day become another need; a new badge of social status, a new diversion, in short yet another necessity. The problem with the dynamic of our present system is that it does not aim to meet needs, material or otherwise, but rather to increase them.

Material needs are too easily satisfied. Diminishing marginal returns soon set in; the first television will be greatly valued, a second may increase our overall satisfaction a little, but a third or fourth will hardly improve anyone's pleasure. The root of our psychological/economic/ecological dilemma is that the present system has to constantly create new needs if it is to keep on going. If we are satisfied, the system collapses through a dearth of consumption, a fall in profits and a slump in investment.

The system demands sharp inequality, so the poor envy and try to catch up with the rich, while the rich try to maintain their position in the hierarchy through consumption. Advertising, marketing and the invention of new kinds of consumer goods keep us on the treadmill. Illich argued that there were two kinds of prisoner in our society, the prisoners of greed and the prisoners of envy.[18] In reality we are all prisoners of an abstract economic system that works only through our dissatisfaction and anguish.

In contrast a Green economy would try to meet material needs without goading us into constantly wanting more. With longer lasting goods, cheap standardized spare parts and sharing we could be the first society in human history to provide prosperity without destroying ourselves or our planet. The economic problem can be solved but only within an ecological society.

Human needs are not just material: the psychologist Maslow introduced the useful idea of a hierarchy of needs, with the material basics at the bottom and psychological needs at the top. A Green economy would work if it motivated individuals by meeting such higher needs in the same way that Smith's model set out to meet the lower ones. One such need is for creative work. Work needs to be redefined and alienating labour reduced. As Slater has noted, 'Many dubious activities in our society . . . are justified on the grounds that they create jobs for people. But why would someone want to work at a monotonous and soul-eating assembly-line job producing something unnecessary or dangerous or destructive? (After all, heroin also creates jobs for people and the work is more interesting.)'[19] A guaranteed income plus the opportunity to produce through community capital would reduce the need for formal work. Ted Trainer justifies the idea of a one-day working week, arguing that having made things to last longer and be easier to repair at home, we will only need to work in the formal sense for a fraction of our time. Informal work would become economically significant and give its own rewards. We could fill our time with a spectrum of exciting activities: learning, thinking, making music, writing, creating, gardening, painting, tinkering with engines, making our goods as we want them and building our own local communities – instead of just working. A Green economy, by reducing formal work, increasing the scope for self-activity and allowing us to use our free time how we wish, would motivate a great many people.

Erich Fromm argued that if people do anti-social or boring work they will tend to compensate through consumption.[20] Alan Roberts feels that if we had more control over our lives and work, we would consume less, in turn reducing the need to work for money in the usual sense.[21] We could stop functioning as economic categories and start living.

In a Green economy work would have a variety of roles, acting not just as a way of meeting material needs, but allowing us to use and develop our skills in a creative way. It would help us to interact co-operatively with others and provide for society as a whole – not just for isolated individuals at the expense of everyone else. A Buddhist work ethic would replace the Protestant code of slavery – an ethic that would, according to Schumacher, 'give a man a chance to utilize and develop his faculties; to enable him to overcome his egocentredness by joining with other people in common tasks; and to bring forth the goods and services needed for a becoming existence . . . To organise such work in such a manner that it becomes meaningless, boring, stultifying, or nerve-wracking for the worker would be little short of criminal; it would indicate a greater concern with goods than with people, an evil lack of compassion and a soul-destroying degree of attachment to the most primitive side of this wordly existence.'[22] Such an ethic should be extended to women as well (an area in which classical Buddhism is strikingly deficient!).

We have social needs; we need other human beings. A Green economy would cut through the Gordian knot of planning versus the market by promoting a social economy based on human co-operation. Most tribal groups had a mechanism whereby the whole community could get together to build homes or bring the crops in. Stonehenge was built without what we would understand as wage labour or state planning. In the film *Witness* there is a remarkable scene where dozens of the Amish villagers get together to build a huge barn. One self-sufficiency network which functioned around Cambridge in the 1970s was described to me in glowing terms. People got together every Sunday, to share their labour, building out-houses, digging fields, planting crops, minimizing effort and maximizing satisfaction. Vast and delicious communal meals were prepared and children 'crèched' while the work was going on. Questions of what to produce, how to produce and for whom to produce could be made increasingly through personal contact instead of bureaucratic decree or market mechanism.

A Green economy would work by combining formal planning with some market mechanisms, going beyond the traditional divide with a growing non-monetized, co-operative sector. As the environmental crisis bites and the present craze for the market tarnishes, the attractions of a new kind of economy will grow. The alternative is constantly increasing destruction, repression and inequality, with an elite minority of paid workers living on top of a workfared majority doing the dirty jobs in return for small amounts of social security payments. Even Conservatives will find it difficult to convince the poor to become poorer to save the rich. In the end we will all sink or swim together. A Green economy is both possible and likely to be popular; other scenarios are unlikely to have either virtue.

Our present economy works only if large numbers of people believe in it. The material structure is underpinned by a behaviourial base. Slater noted that 'it has value only as long as we collectively believe that it does . . . We might say that the 70s raised the same doubts about money that the eighteenth century raised about religion. Money is like the fairy in Peter Pan: if you stop believing in it, it sickens and dies.'[23] We have to start believing in something else.

# 6
# Belief

To root out the real causes of the crisis one has to go beyond economics. Economic processes, even though they affect political events, are underpinned by belief systems without which they could not function. Economics is the study of collective, concentrated psychology. Medieval economics rested on the assumption of just price, rejecting not only usury but also inflation as a sin. The free market was founded on the idea of self-interest. A Green economy would work by generalizing different ideas. Ideas are after all important. Economics, rather than being the sole determining factor, is itself determined.

## The belief system

Much of the psychological substructure that holds up our present destructive society is hidden or so internalized that its elements are no longer seen as concepts that can be accepted or rejected but as common sense closed from debate. The Situationists argued that we exist in a society of the 'spectacle' looking at the world through ideologically tinted glasses; spectacles that we forget we are wearing and confuse with our own sight mechanism. The Italian philosopher and Marxist Antonio Gramsci felt that much of what we take to be obvious or 'human nature' is part of a 'moral hegemony' or set of ideas put in place to support the status quo.

Certainly many of our economic conceptions are hegemonic or 'spectacular'. We could behave in a very different way but our economic behaviour is constrained by an ideological strait-jacket. Growth is the goal, sufficiency is naïve. Some people have eight cars, others have no clean water. Alienating work is accepted as are hierarchies. Our values are not merely superior, they are the only ones possible. Alternative ways of behaving would go against 'human nature' and are 'utopian'. Conventional politicians and economists argue that Greens reject economic 'progress'. Hegemonies are used to build fences around what is possible, to construct divisions between the realistic and the unrealistic. Hegemonies establish the boundaries between what is possible in one kind of society and the ideas that would create a new society with a new reality.

Hegemonies are thus a means of control. According to Gramsci societies are ruled through ideas rather than force; consent not coercion. Rather than putting down discontent it is better to prevent it occurring by moulding common sense into a system of beliefs that support the status quo, subtly preventing discord rather than brutally putting it down. Huxley captures something of its nature in his introduction to *Brave New World*; 'Government by clubs and firing squads, by artificial famine, mass imprisonment and mass deportation, is not merely inhuman (nobody cares much about that nowadays); it is demonstrably inefficient . . .'[1] He goes on to note that a population that loves its servitude is far easier to control. The slaves cease to recognize their bondage for, as Lukes reminds us,

> Is it not the supreme and most insidious exercise of power to prevent people, to whatever degree, from having grievances by shaping their perceptions, cognitions, and preferences in such a way that they accept their role in the existing order of things, either because they can see or imagine no alternative to it, or because they value it as divinely ordained and beneficial.[2]

We are far from being slaves but we forget our power even in a society which is supposed to be free; to vote for radical alternatives, to use our influence as consumers, to change our ideas or withdraw our collective consent from a state that functions only if we allow it to. We all have influence if we seek to use it but feelings of apathy and powerlessness are nurtured by all hegemonies.

There are other elements of hegemony that prevent us achieving a more humane and ecological order. Technological fixes become the answer to social or ecological problems because we forget that we can go to the root of the problem by reducing wasteful consumption or challenging bureaucracy rather than having better filters or a slightly more humane hierarchy. We feel that humankind is innately aggressive, that self-interest is inevitable, that we live in the best of all possible worlds and cannot imagine other ways of being.

But as numerous anthropologists and psychologists have testified one of the few aspects of 'human nature' that can be pinned down is our diversity or lack of any one 'nature'. There have been different economies, some using market mechanisms, others feudal arrangements or tithing, some that promoted gift sharing, co-operation and collective means of distributing goods and services. Different societies have existed with very different values and beliefs from our own.

Many of our present assumptions need to be challenged, brought out into the open, and shown to be part of a belief system rather than simply human nature. We need to regain the right to choose. Equally what is seen as 'natural' or deep seated can be co-opted, distorted, magnified or obscured by the prevailing hegemony. In this sense Green politics is the hegemonic project to end all hegemonic projects. We need to point out that even our most fundamental ideas are still only ideas. Instead of instituting an alternative Green hegemonic yoke, we need to be free of control from above over our thoughts and actions. This does not mean taking on board complete moral relativism or rejecting the idea of those contracts and conventions between individuals that make relationships easier. It does mean though that we should examine where our ideas have come from and reject them if they are found to be destructive or undesirable; moving from false certainties to real choice.

## *Dukkha* and alienation

There is one aspect of human psychology that goes beyond social and ideological conditioning. This is the Buddhist concept of *dukkha*, loosely translated as 'unsatisfactoriness' or 'suffering'. Human beings will never be completely satisfied by life. Not having something, we are unhappy. Getting it and finding that it is not what we want is worse. Reaching a state where we have nothing to strive for and no room for growth because we have achieved all our goals is an even greater form of suffering.

*Dukkha* is a product of change and is sometimes even translated as 'impermanence'. We are always striving for certainty in a world where everything changes. We all grow old, we all eventually die, we all at some point suffer physical or mental anguish. Everything is conditional and subject to change and decay.

The Christian response to *dukkha* (dressed up as original sin) is to look towards the achievement of an unchanging and uncorrodable heavenly kingdom. Gnostics and other early Christians strongly emphasized the evil and putrefying character of the earthly realm, and celebrated the virgin birth of Christ; a spark of spiritual light with little or no connection with stinking humanity or chaotic nature. They looked forward to the swift return of the Messiah and a final victory of spirit over gross matter. But the unchanging and perfect is also the dead and the sterile.

Lynn White Jr has seen Marxism, with its long series of Hegelian steps towards a classless society where alienation and dialectic conflict have been banished, as yet another Christian heresy.[3] Although this may be an exaggerated position, we should beware all who seek perfection in a world which, though improvable, is far from perfectable.

Lewis Mumford shows how Pharaohs tried to achieve such deathless perfection by building pyramids.[4] But while both their bodies and their mausoleums have turned to dust, their spirit lives on; even today if we cannot live for ever we attempt to build monuments or reputations that will. Military conquest, colonialism, the building of business or political dynasties, and the construction of the Channel tunnel can all be seem as part of this 'Kilroy was here' syndrome. Such forms of monument building are an obvious source of conflict, ecological damage and injustice.

The notion of progress is a hegemonic formation, but one based on this fear of death and bound up with the need for permanence. Material expansion and technological development onwards and upwards have become the secular equivalents to Christian notions of the millennium, the apocalypse and the heavenly kingdom. Progress has become a subtle way of justifying the destruction of nature for new roads or dams, the enslavement or wholesale slaughter of native peoples and the need for continual economic expansion whatever the cost.

Far from being a solution, such growth masks the real problem; the more we have (food, consumer durables, land, power) the more we 'need'. Capitalism is at least in part a product of *dukkha*. Without tackling the problem of *dukkha* head on, humanity will never solve the ecological crisis or its fundamental economic problem.

Buddhism like Marxism sees the first (and most important) stage of problem solving in terms of analysis or enlightenment, through the examination of the formerly hidden. To tackle *dukkha*/alienation, we must first admit its existence (like that of hegemony and capitalism). We must see it has another side. Life can be never be in any final sense totally satisfactory; *dukkha* is literally the cost of living. And although it is a cost, it is surely one that is worth paying. The knowledge that there is no permanence, no heavenly kingdom and no utopia, is in itself a way of overcoming dissatisfaction rather than being determined by it. Being aware or enlightened with regard to the problem of *dukkha* we can start to work on our urges to assert ourselves over others, build monuments or over-consume.

## Pyramids and straight lines

Another obstacle to ecological and social harmony is the concept of hierarchy that makes us feel powerless and sets us up above nature. Present society, despite its superficial egalitarianism, makes a great virtue of hierarchy. All societies have had elders, but from the beginning of feudalism, through to our present technocracy, Western society has made a particular virtue of separating humanity from nature, animals from people, men from women and placing just a few men on top of the grand edifice. In a theocratic society the divine right of kings sufficed, in a technological order the cult of the expert has now become the excuse for robbing us of power and the right to self-determination.

Instead of seeing creation as a pyramid with modern man on top, we should remember that there have been past societies superior to our own in many respects, that other species have as much right to exist as *Homo sapiens* and that male values have brought us to a state where we threaten our own survival and that of life on Earth in general. We need to live with our insecurity and, however difficult the task, we must promise not to build pyramids whether intellectual, social or material.

Others have criticized the linear thinking that is a basis of notions of hierarchy and 'progress'. The new physics and elements from oriental religions have helped us to build models of reality which are less reductionist and more holistic, conditional instead of solid. As the physicist and political writer Fritjof Capra notes,

> One of the most difficult things for people in our culture to understand is the fact that if you do something that is good, then more of the same will not necessarily be better. This, to me, is the essence of ecological thinking.[5]

Greens are accused of irrationality by defenders of the status quo, particularly scientists. But in such circumstances scientific rationality can in turn be rejected as irrational or at least deficient because more often than not it tries to portray political problems as technical ones. It is 'irrational' to oppose nuclear power because the 'Third World' needs energy to grow food (scientists often claim), yet is it rational to ignore the problem of cash crops, the irrelevance of large scale Western style development to the needs of the hungry and the dangers of nuclear power? Protesters at public inquiries often have no access to funding or specialized advice because they are perceived to be 'anti-scientific'; then, in a sweeping fulfilment of self-prophecy, they are shown to be without detailed verifiable technical data to back up their arguments. Some technologists would reduce politics to management, Greens must reveal technique as ideology if they are to transform the dominant managerial ideology that is destroying life on Earth.

Other elements of the present hegemony are also under attack. The boundaries of what is 'realistic' have been extended by civil rights activists, the women's movement, gays and lesbians and others. The animal liberation movement has shown us that we are not the only species on this planet. Pacifists have challenged notions of innate aggression and Gandhi showed how it was possible to overcome force through *ahimsa* or non violence. Surrealism and science fiction have shown that even thoughts and visual perceptions demand reconsideration. Ideas are changing on both a popular level and intellectually, yet the growth of hegemonic alternatives remains confused and uncertain.

## The mental means of production

Despite such challenges, more people read *The Sun* or watch MTV (the US video channel) than have ever heard of Gramsci or Green politics. Those who challenge the belief system remain isolated and peripheral. Marx's dictum that 'The ideas of the ruling class are, in every age, the ruling ideas,' remains true to this day. 'The class which has the means of material production at its disposal, has control at the same time over the means of mental production, so that in consequence the ideas of those who lack the means of mental production are, in general, subject to it.'[6] Alternative hegemonic projects are isolated or neutralized. Radical groups have a minute amount of space to put forward ideas throught the education system, media or at election time. Social democratic politicians work with the prevailing hegemony to try to gain votes and respectability instead of seeking to change it. Feminists are marginalized and their opinions are either ridiculed or reproduced in a capitalist model that promotes the career woman instead of the human being. Green politics is sanitized into environmentalism and sold as yet another commodity. Gay pride marches and CND protests justify the system as pluralistic and liberal without giving gays or CND supporters any real power. Protest is put into a quiet corner where democracy can be seen to be done without 'ordinary' people perceiving its impotence.

Most individuals are unfamiliar with the niceties of physics and philosophy, the latest from the Parisian post-Structuralists or the theories of the new, new left. Ideas can be trapped by intellectuals. To have any real effect they need to be released to millions. But it is difficult to see how this will happen. Newspapers and network TV are funded through advertising revenue and remain the prisoners of commerce. Media moguls like Robert Maxwell and Rupert Murdoch compete for monopoly control of magazines, daily papers, publishing houses, satellite television and cable networks. Education is seen as a way of making us fit for work instead of something valuable in its own right.

Physical factors also influence beliefs and prevent challenging ideas from being heard. Higher education cuts, the introduction in Britain of student loans and the promotion of career orientated degrees are likely to make arts, politics and literature courses increasingly rare. Through the sale of council houses, the destruction of working class communities and the extension of share ownership, Mrs Thatcher has tried to develop a material basis for an enhanced and modernized capitalist hegemony that stands in total opposition to Green thinking.

## Challenging hegemony

Such changes have injected a little life into the traditional insurrectionary models of changes. Some might argue that the 'mental means of production' might be seized through revolutionary struggle or by an enlightened future government. In the long term the community should control the media and other sources of information and education but in the short, Greens must start building hegemonic alternatives as well as political and economic ones. One of the reasons the Greens and allied alternative groups have been so successful in Germany is the publication of *Die Tageszeitung*, a radical daily newspaper.[7] At a more modest level local groups might produce parish or estate newsletters putting forward new ideas in a down to earth and palatable form and asking for feedback. Pirate radio is another possibility. Street theatre is a means of challenging hegemony with the pantomime cow being butchered outside McDonald's or the government minister reacting to the motorway his colleague plans to cut through his estate. One danger identified by Frankel is the privatization of culture with individuals retreating to their videos and forgetting neighbours, the environment and wider social changes.[8] But videos can be made by anyone with access to relatively cheap equipment that can often be borrowed officially or otherwise from a community group or college. Greens have to use new forms of media; the street corner meeting may be dead, but other channels of communication live on. While often uninspiring left journals and newspapers see falling sales, a radical comic book like *Crisis* whose first issue looked at the way multinationals are starving the 'Third World' have become increasingly popular and increasingly subversive to the prevailing hegemony.[9]

Popular music is far more important as a means of changing

ideas than books like this will ever be. From Bob Dylan and John Lennon to the Sex Pistols and Michelle Shocked, rock and folk music have become ways of introducing radical ideas to large audiences. I was pleased to be able to speak between bands from the main stage at the Glastonbury Festival in 1989 to appeal for action against the Poll Tax, support for direct action against animal abuse and against compromise in the struggle to save life on Earth. Band Aid, Live Aid, the Mandela birthday celebrations have all, whatever their deficiencies, made millions of people think however superficially about political realities that otherwise would have escaped them. The legendary anarcho-punk band Crass deserve an approving mention at this point. Both Red and Green Wedge tours have been successful in Britain. Popular music can, though, become a substitute for popular action. Protest music can take the place of protest (and the construction of alternatives). Youth cults based on such music may become a way of dividing groups from each other within society. Massive record companies increasingly rely on safe formulas and have no interest in encouraging social change.

Art can be used as a tool for change, opening up minds and shocking individuals into considering their often unconsidered views. Cultural events such as benefits and festivals can be used as a way of propagating alternative ideas, raising funds and of increasing group cohesion.

Elections should be used as an opportunity for changing not just voting habits but ideas. Canvassing, effective leaflets, public debates and creative use of the media all help to move people. Die Grünen produce hundreds of poster designs which are accessible to everyone with simple but often subversive messages. A pink washed photograph of Kohl's cabinet with just one woman in view is titled 'The future of women's politics?'. On another a seal appeals to humans to stop dumping their rubbish in the North Sea. Designs deal with sexual politics, government scandals, organic farming, workers' rights and a host of other issues – they are uniformly a delight to the eye as well as a tool for change.

The belief system is far from uniform and has a stronger hold on some individuals than others; different sub-belief systems dominate various sectors of society. We don't live in an ideological 'bloc' or monolith; islands of cloth-capped traditional labour movement socialism survive in a few rare locations. Many people still hold, consciously or unconsciously, to the post-war Keynesian consensus that mixed both the market and socialism. Thatcherism as a distinct set of somewhat contradictory ideas on the one hand celebrating the dynamism of the free market and on the other a support for authority and traditional values has widespread, but far from total, support. There are growing pockets of alternative awareness. Bahro has argued on many occasions that while five per cent of people were already Green, five per cent of the consciousness of the rest was Green and that no one should be abandoned as lost. The trick will be to challenge, without alienating, very different types of people with different levels of understanding and sympathy.

Green parties and community groups should put resources into political education, making sure that all members and supporters understand the basis of Green politics and the need for alternatives. Political ideas cannot be brought down from on high by prophets; they need to be discussed as widely as possible and clearly thought through. Superficial environmentalism does not get to the roots political, psychological or economic of the environmental crisis. If we care about life on Earth, we need to go beyond environmentalism. While ideas should be articulated in a way which doesn't alienate the audience, Green politics has to challenge, going beyond what is electorally safe.

## Spiritual change

So far even Greens have acted in a fairly grey way. The communes, city farms and alternative technology projects set up in the 60s and 70s have largely collapsed. The Green movement in Germany has been marked by conflict, factional argument and disharmony. If the Greens 'cannot act as brothers, what hope is there for the rest of us for the future?'[10] Yet it is not enough to wake up and suddenly say from now on, 'I will cease to be egotistical, argumentative, greedy or over-assertive.' In a patriarchal society, it is difficult for women to get involved in politics and gain confidence and competence. Organizations like the 300 Group who want to see an equal number of women MPs to men in the UK parliament have enormous value but it is *men* that need to radically change their behaviour and the practices that work to exclude women. In a society where we learn to defer to fathers, head masters, scientists and bureaucrats, it is no wonder that 'apathy' is so rife. We have no real chance of behaving or believing in a Green way until we live in a Green society, where we have been brought up, educated and allowed to work within structures very different from those we have now. The paradox is obvious; to reach a new society, we have to act with the kind of values that are only truly possible within the kind of society we are striving for. One way of overcoming the paradox and leaping the gap is through spiritual/psychological change; emphasizing the need for internal as well as external revolution.

We should not seek escape; nor must we accept 'New Ageism' that substitutes personal for political change. Spiritual/psychological change is impossible without political/material movement. Fromm argued that spiritual and social action were closely linked and demanded disciplined practice over a long period. Spiritual practice may be inspired by the notion of God or Gaia, whether through Islam or a host of other religious traditions. But changing ourselves should not mean that we have to worship charismatic gods or gurus or bow down before Pan. Traditions including Quakerism, some types of Paganism, Taoism, and the humanistic Marxism pioneered by Fromm can help us grow without demanding unthinking obedience.[11] Buddhism which tries to gently root out greed and violence is useful because it works through straightforward and relatively simple practice. Using Buddhist techniques does not mean that we have to follow or cease to follow any other more formal set of spiritual ideas. Buddhism stresses the need for both compassion and awareness. Compassion means understanding that we are connected to our environment, to other individuals and to other species; that there is no absolute division between us and the outside. If we hurt what we take to be outside us, we hurt ourselves. Such compassion will only be effective when combined with awareness both psychological and political. A variety of spiritual or psychological schools stress the need for wakefulness; most of the time we act as if we are asleep, controlled by the prevailing sentiments of our society, prey to our emotions and only partially in control of our own destinies. To borrow from Gurdjieff, we need to fight a war against sleep, concentrating hard enough to break through the dreams engendered by the prevailing hegemony. Political and personal change depends on sharpening our awareness of the workings of our selves and of the structures with which we interact. We cannot seek to change ourselves or our society unless we first understand what we are trying to change.

The danger is that through spiritual practice we may seek personal solace rather than work for political change. Meditation can become just another ego trip. Spiritual practice can only succeed as part of a collective effort with the mutual support of others seeking to challenge the present order of things in a deep-seated way. It needs to go hand in hand with a political strategy that changes society in a structural way, so as to make psychological progress easier. Violence and sudden insurrection contradict such progress. We need to win others over instead of fighting them. Racism, nationalism and class loyalties are used to make soldiers see their enemies as separate and non-human. Radical pacifist strategies try to break down the alienation and show that we are all the same. If we stereotype our opponents, we will fail to nurture the five per cent of their consiousness that may already be challenging the prevailing belief system. Difficult as it is, we need to develop strategies that subvert rather than destroy.

## Models of insurrection

The kind of violent, October 1917-type Revolution described by Gramsci as war of manoeuvre needed, in his eyes, to be replaced with a process whereby the majority of the population is won over to a hegemonic alternative through what was described as a war of position. He compared such a strategy to that of trench warfare with the opposing army gradually building up its forces (in a largely non-violent way) before advancing on the enemy.

Arguably Greens and others have been involved in a long war of position since the sixties, putting forward a distinct set of ideas which challenge the roots of capitalism far more fundamentally than do those of the traditional left. The challenge is a broad one linking together feminists, the new left, environmentalists and many others. Subjects as diverse as architecture, sexuality and medicine are under discussion. Certainly new ideas are becoming more popular on both an academic and at a broader level. The Greens have a clear hegemonic position that no other political force in the Western World other than the radical right possesses. Such a position will not automatically succeed; in a slow war of position, the ruling class possesses most of the resources and is in a strong position to slowly wear down the alternative. Trench warfare, if finally successful, may even be too slow to save the planet.

Greens, in contrast to this approach, need to indulge in a bold strategy of philosophical guerrilla warfare; exploding concepts of self-interest, sexism and hierarchy as well as introducing new options. *The Ecologist* magazine has indulged in such a strategy since the early 1970s with great success, challenging nuclear power, the value of economic growth and reductionism in science (although it has been less concerned with combatting sexism and hierarchy). The philosophical guerrilla should identify contradictions and push them into their opposites. Capitalism promises prosperity yet millions particularly in the developing world live in poverty. Despite wealth millions of others feel their lives to be pointless and boring. Despite freedom of choice we have little say in decision making. Despite the 'free market', multinationals call the tune. To achieve short term economic 'security', we are destroying life. Contradictions can be made more obvious and the owners of 'the mental means of production' put on the defensive.

Gramsci also examined the need to turn *passive* revolution (described earlier in terms of negative feedback, whereby the system changes to effectively stay the same) into its opposite of *active* revolution (or positive feedback, where the system changes radically and becomes something new). One way of achieving this goal is to tempt the creators of hegemony into positions which they cannot defend or from which they have to reject what they seek to defend. Philosophical guerrillas need to embarrass and overbalance their opponents. Mrs Thatcher's 'conversion' to Green has placed her in a very delicate position, because while her government continues to build nuclear power stations, opposition to nuclear waste dumping has been made legitimate in the eyes of her former supporters. One Tory MP remarked that Mrs Thatcher's use of the word 'Green' gave the Green Party thousands of extra votes in the 1989 European elections and that the term should be banned from the lips of Conservative politicians. The UK government urges developing countries to grow their way out of crisis, effectively asking them to ignore the poor and chop down the rainforests to maximize exports of cash crops and mineral commodities. At the same time the Overseas Development Administration has increased its funding for rainforest protection. In the end ecology is incompatable with economic expansion, and social justice is alien to the pursuit of profit. Ruling ideas can be broken and made to look pathetic.

Greens must politicize the depoliticized. For example, diet is not just a matter of personal habit but a product of decisions made by giant companies who profit from lax standards, high fat content and large numbers of additives. International poverty is explained not as something political and economic but as a product of natural disasters, poor climate and local incompetence. Non-political perceptions of domestic poverty in the 'first world' look likely to follow. Instead of giving, we need to stop taking through arms sales, low commodity prices and the exploitation of cheap 'Third World' labour. In the film *Apocalypse Now* one character remarks grittily, 'We cut them in half with machine guns and then give them band aid.'

Greens need to look at the most basic and fundamental aspects of our lives that are blighted by the system within which we live, and show that our surroundings, health, housing and numerous related issues are political problems that demand political solutions.

## Argument is not enough

Beliefs don't function in a vacuum. The material – our environment, work, leisure, architecture, etc. – affects the mental. In turn, ideas shape our material surroundings, the values of Peter Palumbo or Prince Charles leading to very different types of built environment. It is not enough to change the world through argument as liberals believe, or purely through the material, as a vulgar Marxist would claim. There is a constant dialectic; we have to do both. There are no clear triggers for change, economics is determined by particular assumptions but these assumptions are influenced by economic, political and structural factors. Discussion of ultimate causes, of base versus superstructure, has become more of an academic chicken and egg debate than a guide to action.

To achieve change we have the choice of working in an enormous variety of ways. Power is not a carefully hidden jewel for which we have to go through a long dungeon and dragons type of political quest. It is certainly not a product of the parliamentary system alone. Some people have more power than others, but their greatest source of strength comes from telling the rest of us that we are powerless. Whether within formal political parties, in community groups, at our place of work or through financial pressure, we have the power to change society. We need to become *aware* of our power, get *together* with others and start *using* it to the greatest effect possible. Positive political change has always been about the struggle for justice; without justice, survival for all peoples, all classes and perhaps all species will be impossible.

It won't be easy. The difference between carrying on business as usual and working for a different society is the difference between the very difficult and the impossible. Everyone has a part to play in transforming society. Starting from wherever we are and doing whatever we feel most necessary, we must keep going till we get there. The future is either Green or not at all. There is no alternative. Over to you.

# Opening up the dialogue

This book will not have served its purpose if it does not stimulate discussion and debate. To start the ball rolling, three people who are active and articulate in the Green movement have agreed to comment on *Getting There*, and each in their own way has taken the arguments a step further. Their contributions are on the following pages.

**Mary Mellor** teaches sociology at Newcastle Polytechnic, and is a member of the Socialist Environment and Resources Association (SERA). As this book goes to press, she is writing a book on feminist green socialism for Virago. She has written on green politics, feminism and co-operatives.

**Ted Trainer** teaches sociology at the University of New South Wales, and is a supporter of alternative projects and radical lifestyle change. He has written two books on the need for ecological transformation in relation to development issues: *Abandon Affluence!* (Zed Books, 1985) and *Developed to Death* (Green Print, 1989).

**Peter Tatchell** is a member of the Labour Party and SERA, and a leading light in the campaign for a red-green convergence. He has articulated a strategy for a 'united green and socialist Europe', and is a sympathetic critic of the Green Party. He also campaigns widely for lesbian and gay liberation, radical medicine and non-provocative defence strategies. His books include *Democratic Defence: a non-nuclear alternative* (GMP, 1985) and *AIDS: A guide to survival* (GMP, 1987).

# Ecology, socialism and feminism

*Mary Mellor*

This book launches a debate that is essential and long overdue. For nearly two hundred years the political economy of the West has rested on the expansionary assumptions of industrial capitalism; its commitment to growth and development has been reflected in philosophies and programmes across the political spectrum. The present ecological crisis undermines these assumptions to such an extent that we need to rethink political economy from first principles. In the face of resource depletion and environmental degradation, collective and socially just action is the only possible basis for an humane response, but if we have not managed to build socialism in an age of plenty (albeit relative and geographically limited), how will we achieve it in an age of scarcity?

In trying to answer this question, Derek Wall writes as a green reaching out to the heritage of socialism. I write as a socialist who recognizes the challenge of the green critique to that heritage. Both of us would wish to argue the case for a green socialism but we cannot assume a natural compatibility of the two positions. Derek argues that the green movement has four basic principles: ecology, decentralization, non-violence and social justice. This marks a difference of emphasis from the four 'pillars' of the German Green Party: ecology, grassroots democracy, non-violence and social responsibility (Parkin, 1989, p. 120). The political direction of the green movement and the prospect for green socialism depends on the crucial distinction between the personally-based idea of social responsibility and the collectively-based idea of social justice. This question has yet to be adequately tackled within the Green Parties. The English translation of the 1983 Programme of Die Grünen only talks of a 'social' principle under which they declare themselves 'against a work process ruled by economic power' but their solution is individual, based on self-determination and human and democratic rights.

The political question at the heart of the attempt to build a green socialism is whether the possibility of social change rests in the structures of 'society' or in the hearts or minds of people. In the end the conclusion of this book is that it is both; a dialectical relationship in which they are two sides of the same coin. Green socialism would place local initiatives within a framework of regional, national and global regulation/co-ordination. Such an arrangement is problematic in terms of potential conflict and political control. Conflict will emerge between autonomous local initiatives and the regulating bodies if they are not operating from the same basic principles. In England, for instance, it would be impossible to set up local initiatives through a 'green dollar' scheme as it is illegal to issue currency. Even regulation to prevent ecological destruction may undermine local autonomy and cause deprivation, such as the banning of such local practices as peat-cutting, slash-and-burn agriculture, seal culling or the killing of pilot whales.

Decentralization and autonomy within a regulatory structure depends upon who controls those structures, how they are made up and who makes the decisions. We need to establish ecologically sustainable and socially just co-ordinating structures while retaining the possibility for local control of collective action. Green socialism has to find a route from the present political and economic structures that destroy the environment, *through* forms of decentralized protest that can establish autonomous structures, *to reach* a situation where global institutions can co-operatively and justly regulate human impact upon the environment. The danger of the current situation is that partial solutions will be developed by 'experts' that deny social justice or autonomy, or that there is a political hijack such as Margaret Thatcher's espousal of nuclear power in response to the greenhouse effect. This book starts to build the kind of political analysis and programme that will tackle these problems and while I welcome much of the discussion, I have some reservations, mostly from a feminist perspective.

In the early part of the book criticism is levelled at a variety of targets: industrialism, science, technology, masculinity, political parties – but overwhelmingly capitalism and more specifically capitalist economics and the question of growth. Most of the discussion is directed to the problems of raw material extraction and manufacturing and its ecological impact. However capitalism also exploits 'invisible' trades; banking, insurance or services, education, health, beauty therapy, analysis, law. The crisis of over-production and the impetus to growth was very much a problem of manufacturing, a crisis of the need to cover the costs of large capital investments. This is not such a problem for a £100 'off the shelf' company with a letter head and a mail drop. An attack on the structures of capitalism must dissociate those aspects that can be attacked from an ecological perspective and those that can be attacked from a socialist perspective.

This is a difficult area that raises questions as to whether the ecological crisis favours a socialist solution or indeed if a green position is inherently socialist? I would answer 'no' to both questions. This does not mean that we should not fight to build a green socialism; but we cannot assume it will somehow 'emerge'. The car industry, for example, is anathema from an ecological perspective but in Europe and North America it formed the basis of mass production and mass consumption that incorporated the working class and gave it what little (short-lived) benefit it has had from industrial capitalism. Loan sharking is plainly a problem from a socialist perspective but has no immediate environmental impact. By the same token the green movement cannot assume that ecological questions will automatically produce a 'green' response in other areas. A green case is made for holistic medicine but as traditional medicine cannot be claimed to be hugely environmentally damaging arguments have to be raised on other grounds. Holistic treatment could be equally costly in human labour and training and could easily be as exploitative and undemocratic as privatized traditional medicine.

In our attack on industrial capitalism and growth we must identify those areas that are directly ecologically damaging and try to predict what the response of the present socio-economic structure is likely to be in the face of scarcity of raw materials, lack of clean water, and nowhere to dump wastes. We have to look at the options the 'enemy' has, for example, stock-piling, raising prices, or moving into ecologically acceptable areas such as water filters, alternative technology, or additive-free food. Capital has proved itself to be a very adaptable system and we must not underestimate it. Eco-fascism is a real possibility too. We are also hampered by the fact that both traditional and Marxist economics have given far too much credence to industrial capitalism and its theoretical justification. Economics is, as Derek Wall states, 'a collective concentrated psychology'; it is not a science. It is also a process that has systematically excluded and marginalized women, which brings me to my main quarrel with this book.

Derek shares with many writers in both the green and socialist tradition a lack of awareness of the reality of women's lives. Reference is made to the 'women's movement', 'feminism' and 'sexism' but the thrust of his argument is entirely from the 'public' male-oriented sphere of economic and political life. The economic system he attacks is male-dominated, women only enter at the periphery as highly exploited and vulnerable wage labour. Largely overlooked in this book are domestic labour, and caring for the young, the sick, the elderly. This leads him to conclude that because people in America will not spend longer than 15 minutes preparing a meal, they will be too lazy to sort refuse. He does not consider that it is women, often in waged labour, who are refusing to spend hours preparing food. Not lazy, just sick of the double-shift. Women may well be more than happy to spend the time saved sorting their rubbish. Another lack of awareness of the politics of women's position is the reference to a 'domestic gift economy', again a phrase used in other texts. In patriarchal society, women's domestic labour is more slavery than 'gift'. Oddly, Derek uses the phrase to refer to *communal exchange* rather than domestic work.

Derek rightly argues for the need to exploit small spaces, to find areas of autonomy to begin the fight-back. He recommends local initiatives such as learning exchanges, green fairs, skills exchanges, cycle ways, flexible work patterns, ethical investment trusts, city farms, organic food networks, co-operatives, decentralized services. These represent 'public' areas of communal and economic life; they do not cover the private world of domestic work and caring. Green socialism must break down these artificial boundaries and bring caring and child-rearing into public view. Women do not have autonomy but they do have whole areas of their life that capitalism has not yet reached, *but is invading*. I would wish to argue that the failure of the socialist attack on capital is that it has been conducted from within capital's own framework of production and commodified exchange which identifies what is to be seen as 'economic' and to be given a 'value' or a 'worth'. A hungry child, an incontinent parent, a handicapped or sick person cannot wait for the market to respond or a politician to decide if they can 'afford' to provide a service. This is not the reality of women's lives; women respond immediately without 'reward' or a 'policy initiative'. Lack of awareness of such basic activities, that need to be done day in day out, is reflected in Derek's vision of a green socialist future which offers a spectrum of exciting activities: 'learning, thinking, making music, writing, creating, gardening, tinkering with engines(!), making our goods *when we want them*, building our local communities'. These reflect a male view of activities which are all public or 'choice' work. In such an ideally 'free' community, who is changing the soiled sheets?

Apart from this basic criticism I support the thrust of the book that sees political action as a system of 'transitional demands', as even the most innocent attempt to harness waste land or gain access to open spaces can bring down the wrath of vested interests. One notable example was Gandhi's march for salt, when the ludicrous nature of the lack of such a basic right was forcefully brought home by the vicious response he and his followers suffered. I also welcome the fact that this book is free of the mawkish sentimentality that invades some green texts, where nature and spirituality are seen in entirely beneficent terms. We have to understand quite clearly why people sought to conquer nature, how frightening they found its seasons, pests, predators and uncertainties. We must sympathize with why human society felt the need for the control that science and technology offered. One of the benefits of our control of nature is that we feel closer to it; our own products are much more dangerous (Chernobyl). Nature is not 'natural'; it has been constructed by thousands of years of human activity and we can build on that history to create a green and socialist society that is sustainable for future generations.

# The task of education

*Ted Trainer*

Before discussing the problem of transition I would like to highlight aspects of the conserver society to which I believe we have to move, because having these in mind helps to clarify the way the transition might be made.

There is widespread agreement that a just, peaceful and ecologically sustainable society must be built on the concept of small scale, *highly self-sufficient town and suburban economies* in which all the world's people can have a perfectly adequate material living standard and a high quality of life on *very low capita* levels of resource use and GNP. This means living simply, i.e., without affluence and waste, reducing transport and especially international trade, establishing a neighbourhood workshop on each block, and having local committees and working bees perform many functions now controlled by distant bureaucracies. There would be use of alternative technologies, formation of local people's banks that will only lend on socially useful projects in the region, and promotion of a large non-cash sector of the economy in which people could barter and organize co-operative services and give surpluses to each other and take free goods from the communal orchards and ponds and woodlots. Neighbourhoods would be enriched as leisure venues, thus reducing the desire to travel. Especially important would be developing thriving permaculture systems, even in cities, so that most of our food and materials can be produced where people live and the nutrients can then be returned to the soil. Re-zoning would be undertaken to site market gardens, woodlots, aquaculture and orchards right in cities and suburbs. Many unnecessary industries would be phased out. There would be huge reductions in the number of firms since so many are at present producing non-necessities and there would be decentralization of most of the remaining factories and offices. Thus most people could get to work on foot or by bicycle, meaning much less need for the car. Therefore we could dig up many roads and convert them to food production, etc. Neighbourhoods and towns would become increasingly co-operative communities, with much communal property and many functions performed by committees and working bees.

None of this involves any reduction in standards that matter, such as for health care or dental technology or the quality of refrigerators or public transport. High technology research into socially useful items could leap ahead because we would transfer to it the research and development presently wasted on things like sports cars and armaments. There could still be various functions for national systems of government – transport, law, telecommunications – but on nothing like the scale that we have at present. We would then have an economy that was totally different from free enterprise capitalism and 'big-state' socialism/communism, although it would contain elements of both. There would have to be considerable planning and control, but most of this could be carried out by unpaid local committees (e.g., for maintenance of the neighbourhood windmill, the library, the orchards and ponds). There could be many small private 'family' firms, so long as they were not concerned with profit or growth, and there could be a role for market forces although only in specific and monitored areas. Such an economy is best thought of as a Third Way, characterized mainly by as much regional self-sufficiency as possible, so that little is imported into the town because its needs are mostly met by its own labour, capital, land resources and talent. There would also be a large co-operative sector of the economy, a large cashless sector and a large free goods and services sector.

## Assisting escapees

Now given this vision of the goal, it can be seen that central to the transition must be enabling increasing numbers of individuals to move out of the five-day working week, high-cash income, high-consuming way of life into a more relaxed, varied, supportive and co-operative one where they work for cash only one to two days a week and satisfy most of their simple needs by their own production, by barter, by payment in kind and by the many free goods available from the neighbourhood (produced by the one day a week we all give to community work projects). We have to get to the stage where governments can start facilitating the development of such alternative economies within the existing growth-and-greed society, so that the increasing numbers dumped into unemployment by the mainstream economy and the many people bored in conventional jobs can start to move over to the more sane and rewarding way.

## Public awareness: the crucial element

We are at present a very long way from the stage where governments would begin to facilitate the development of highly self-sufficient and largely self-governing small local communities. Thus the crucial task before us now is not trying to make the actual changes in society, but building the public awareness and support that has to be there before any significant change becomes possible. We can get nowhere unless and until most people come to understand a) the unsustainable nature of our society, b) the need for a conserver society, and c) how satisfactory it could be to live in a conserver society. We are probably *decades* away from the point in time when this preliminary goal will have been achieved and there is little sense in trying to get structural and system changes made until this groundwork has been done. Certainly there is value in setting up procedures (such as community gardens) that will be universally used after the transition, but only as educational devices. (See below.) There is little value in just having one more community garden around, as if the more we establish the closer we get to the goal of having them everywhere. They can't be everywhere until people in general understand why they are necessary, and they will not understand that until we have done a lot of explaining. *It is explaining that is crucial, not the establishing of more community gardens.* Just starting them won't by itself get the need for them understood. Of course establishing them can be an excellent device for the educational process, but unless this distinction is clearly in mind lots of energy can go into projects that end up being little more than the hobby obsessions of a small minority and make little or no contribution to educating people in general about the need for a conserver society.

## It is too early for electoral politics

One implication of this view is that it is premature for us to be putting much energy into electoral politics – i.e., into trying to form parties, influence election outcomes, or get green people elected – with a view to having an impact here and now on legislation or government policy. In most cases, even including that of the German Greens, we a very long way from having the numbers to enable us to make any progress at all towards the fundamental changes in society that must be our overriding goal. Consequently our top priority for a long time yet should be to win more and more people to the movement at the grass roots level. Only if we work hard at that for many more years can we eventually expect to have voted in enough political representatives to form the majority, and only then can we begin to get the structural changes through. Of course working now in the electoral arena may be useful as an educational strategy, but one must think very carefully about whether or not that is the most cost-effective option open.

## Fighting bushfires and saving furry animals

Most of the environmental movement's time and energy is going into attempting to protect threatened bits of the environment. Very little of it is going into promoting the transition to a conserver society. In fact it is my firm belief that most members of environmental organizations do not yet understand that radical social change is needed. Consequently one of our urgent tasks is to work within green organizations to get them to rethink their priorities.

Of course there are many environmental bushfire-fighting problems that just have to be attended to immediately and I do not suggest that we should ignore these. However, working to save bits of the environment from destruction *is far from the most important thing to do*. It typically makes no contribution to getting rid of the monster that insists on devouring more and more of the environment. If you save this wild river or that forest the growth economy will just move on to rip up others somewhere else. The top priority of environmental groups should be increasing public understanding of the need for transition to a social system that is not a monster devouring increasing quantities of resources, ecosystems, species and people.

## Personal lifestyle changes or political/educational action?

Another very common mistake is to assume that the transition can be made through individuals changing their personal lifestyles in conserver directions. Such changes are admirable, but far from sufficient and far from the most important goals for our energy to be devoted to. The most crucial changes that have to be made are in social systems and structures. For instance we have to get to the stage where market gardens can be located in cities, many city streets dug up, most petrol stations converted to neighbourhood workshops, and a garbage gas unit installed behind every five to ten houses. These changes to the geography and functioning of our settlements can only be brought about through political action that gets legislation through, and that will only be possible when majorities understand the need for the changes and willingly vote for them. So the top priority should be to work on whatever educational projects are likely to build those majorities. Changing one's own lifestyle will probably make no contribution at all to this goal. This is not an argument against changing one's lifestyle; it is a plea for thinking carefully about what actions are going to contribute to raising the understanding that will lead to change in social structures.

## Does Marx show the way?

No social theory throws anywhere near as much light on why our world has serious problems as does Marx's account of the nature and functioning of capitalism. Most of what is wrong is directly explicable in terms of the terrible contradictions that result because it is not in the interests of the very few who control capital to invest it in meeting the needs of most people or of the planet. However I want to argue that with respect to some central aspects of the transition to a sustainable society, Marx was seriously mistaken.

Marxists typically assume that when we have got rid of capitalism we can release the forces of production, i.e. open the throttles in the factories, so that 'everyone can have a Mercedes.' Many Marxists do not understand that if we phase out capitalism but still insist on having affluent living standards and endless economic growth, we will have just about the same range of catastrophic global problems that we are faced with now. Marx could not have been expected to know it, but the good society cannot be an affluent society.

Similarly Marx believed that a high level of 'development of the productive forces' was essential before a good society became possible, and that according to the 'laws of history' the transition would come only after capitalism had matured and had eventually killed itself off. But conservers and alternative lifestylers know, as do the members of many 'primitive' tribes, the Amish communities and the early Kibbutzim, that only very low living standards and levels of industrialization are necessary for perfectly satisfactory material living conditions and a high quality of life. The good life and the good society do not depend very much on material technology. They are essentially to do with values, expectations and social organization. I know of many people who live quite well materially in Australian communes on below-poverty incomes. In one the per capita cash expenditure per week is \$45. In another it is \$25, around one fifth the national poverty line! Hence it is not at all obvious to conservers that there is any technical need to go through the miseries of capitalism. They can't see why it is in principle impossible for the spread of the right ideas and values to lead people in overdeveloped societies and in underdeveloped societies to switch fairly suddenly to the alternative way. (In fact this seems to have been the position that Marx himself was coming to in the letters he wrote during the last ten years of his life, especially in considering the situation of the Russian peasant collective villages.) In any case we have no choice but to proceed on the assumption that this is possible, because we do not have time to wait for capitalism to grind itself to dust before we can start the transition. The ecosystems of the planet might only have a few decades left.

Marx thought that after capitalism is scrapped there would have to be a long period of dictatorship of the proletariat, in which mistaken ideas like greed and selfishness were overcome, before a collective society could function without any need for a coercive state. But it seems that we must reverse this order of events. Changes in ideas and values have to be achieved *before* any structural change in the direction of a conserver society is possible. You can pull off many sorts of coups and revolutions without public understanding or acceptance but you cannot make a conserver society work unless people understand the need for it, enjoy it and willingly work at it.

It is sad that there is a tendency for our efforts to be weakened by a split between red and green. Both sides must realize that neither has all the answers but both are essential. Greenies often fail to see that capitalism is the source of our problems and that just saving furry animals won't make a significant difference in the long run. Reds often fail to see that just getting rid of capitalism and continuing to pursue affluence and growth won't make much difference either. But both camps have the essential ingredients for a vision that is about a post-capitalist conserver society of self-governing and highly self-sufficient small, green and largely cashless economies.

## Beware the strike by capital

Assuming that we are successful in moving public opinion towards the conserver view, and in getting more alternatives going so that increasing numbers of people can move out of the rat race into the low consuming lifestyle, at some point we will run into our most difficult problem. Sooner or later *capital will go on strike.* When capitalists see that Australia, for example, is trying to turn from the high consumption path, they would at least pull out their capital, if not attempt to crush the whole venture. There is no way of escaping this problem; our only hope is to have done such good preparatory work that when the crunch comes enough Australians will understand the situation and have the necessary commitment for us to get through. It is likely that there would be very hard times and economic and social turmoil as vital industries were closed down and too many people were dumped into unemployment for the new local economies to absorb easily. It is also likely that the chaos would fuel reactionary movements.

However, the important point here is that the alternative way is by definition not very dependent on the things the corporations supply. It does not require many imports, or that much high tech or capital, to make relatively self-sufficient conserver society function well, providing there has been time to get it into shape. Our task therefore is to get ourselves into good enough condition quickly enough to survive this period.

## Getting examples going

It is extremely important that we get as many visible examples of alternative ways functioning as quickly as possible, ready to be used as educational devices. We have far too few illustrations for people to observe and experience. We need to be able to let large numbers of people see for themselves that conserver ways are not just viable but are highly enjoyable. Most effective are fully developed alternative communities that can be visited. There is a desperate need for film and video accounts of what life in these communities is like.

However there is another strategy that is much more accessible to the rest of us who live in fairly ordinary suburbs. A small group can organize a tour of specific alternative technologies and ways that are located in different places throughout the town or suburb. A class of children might go by bus to a house which has solar panels, where aspects of alternative energy are explained, then hop back on the bus to visit someone's organic garden, then a backyard with a mud brick dog kennel and lots of photos of mud brick building. Here and there on the tour there could be many displays, models and objects making theoretical points about the need for a conserver society. Especially useful is a model, or just maps, of the town or suburb showing how it could be made into a more self-sufficient economy.

The next stage in this strategy would be to include activities in which people can actually participate during the tour, such as making some mud bricks, trying a pottery wheel, picking some vegetables for the co-operative lunch, helping to make a solar panel. These are the sort of experiential learnings that are most effective in getting people to realize how satisfying the conserver lifestyle can be.

## We are getting there

Finally, although the road ahead is quite uncertain, we should not forget what miraculous success we have had in a mere 25 years. The curves of awareness and concern have come from the base line in the early 1960s to remarkable levels now. It is just a matter of keeping them accelerating. It might take another 20 years but at some point we will have built the *critical mass* of public opinion that will be sufficient to tip the balance and then the structural changes will start to take place rapidly. My argument has been that the most important contribution to this end can be made by devoting ourselves to the grass roots educational task and being careful not to get drawn into ventures that might be noble, but which do little to raise public awareness of the core themes.

# Strategies for power

*Peter Tatchell*

We are all now aware, at least in a general sense, of the escalating ecological crisis and the parallel rise of green politics.

What Derek Wall has done in this book is to set out many of the specifics of a radical green agenda. Exploring both green political philosophy and green policy prescriptions, he makes an overwhelming case for the necessity and possibility of the ecological transformation of society.

In addition to Derek Wall's discursive articulation of the multi-layered and inter-meshing levels of individual, local, national and global action required to bring about this green conversion of the social order, there is also a need for Greens and their allies to think through specific and concrete strategies for the achievement of political power.

Though changing popular consciousness and mobilizing mass movements is an integral and important part of the transition to an ecological society, mere ideological hegemony and political oppositionism is not enough.

At the end of the day, saving our society and our planet from ecological disaster also requires the parliamentary power necessary to put green policies into practice.

The Westminster and European parliaments are now the principle forums of decision-making which affect the lives and environments of the peoples of England, Scotland and Wales. We must therefore explicitly address the issue of how we can win, and use the political power of these parliamentary institutions to re-orient our societies in a progressive green direction.

In the case of the European Parliament, the victory of the Green and Left parties in the 1989 elections has opened up new opportunities to challenge the right-wing 1992 project of Europe

Plc with an alternative vision of a Green and Socialist Europe which prioritizes commitments to economic democracy and ecological sustainability.

This possibility, which remains as yet unrealized, depends on the willingness of the Left and Green parties in the European Parliament to begin a dialogue and to explore ways of working together. At present, collaboration to transform the European Community is severely limited by the fragmentation and division which exists between the Greens and the Left. Taken individually, both party groupings are in a minority in the European Parliament, though their combined voting strength adds up to a majority. Agreement and co-ordination between Greens and Socialists is therefore essential to enable them to challenge the substantial bloc of Centre-Right MEPs and to reorient the European Parliament around a progressive agenda, including the long overdue strengthening of its own legislative powers.

Sadly, there are plenty of chauvinists and sectarians within both the Left and the Greens who reject political co-operation. They arrogantly presume that their movement alone is the embodiment of progressive ideas and the exclusive instrument of social advance. Such people would rather put their own narrow party interests before cross-party co-operation to win an enlightened Europe.

Despite some very real obstacles to such co-operation, there is much common ground between the Socialist, Green, Communist, independent Left and radical regionalist parties (such as the Basques) in the European Parliament. Indeed, during the 1984–89 European Parliament there was frequent collaboration between MEPs from all these parties on many diverse issues such as health and safety, women's rights, pollution control, AIDS prevention, energy conservation, regional funding, hazardous waste disposal, anti-racism, public transport, animal welfare, freedom of information, homosexual equality, agricultural reform, Third World aid, and workplace democracy.

Most significantly, the Green-Alternative European Link (GRAEL) group of MEPs formed a working alliance between the Belgian and West German Greens, the Italian revolutionary socialists from Democrazia Proletaria, and the Dutch Green Progressive Accord (itself a four-party electoral pact between the Greens, Communists, Radicals and left-wing Pacifist Socialists). This GRAEL group of MEPs was, in turn, part of the larger Rainbow Group which also included the Danish Peoples Movement Against Membership of the European Community, and the European Free Alliance, a left-leaning regionalist bloc of Basque, Flemish and Sardinian MEPs.

Despite their differences, the member parties of GRAEL and the Rainbow Group succeeded in co-operating closely. They consistently established a pace-setting radical agenda within the European Parliament. By so doing, GRAEL and the Rainbow Group pointed the way forward to the new kind of pluralistic politics and broad-based alliances which are critical for Green and Left advance throughout Europe. In the future, similar collaboration between Greens and Socialists is imperative if we are to have any hope of remedying the damaging consequences of the Single European Market with its competitive and productivist rationale, and of averting the danger that the European Community could develop into a centralized and authoritarian West European superpower.

The immediate priority must therefore be to establish a Europe-wide progressive alliance which can reproduce, on a larger scale, the success of GRAEL and the Rainbow Group in bringing together Reds and Greens and articulating a radical programme for the ecological and socialist transformation of the member states.

The basis for this expanded co-operation is the broad agreement that is already emerging between Greens and Socialists, particularly at grassroots level, on key strategic issues such as environmental conservation and sustainable economics, industrial democracy and consumer protection, job creation and minimum income, decentralization and regional autonomy, human rights and equal opportunities, disarmament and non-provocative defence, and international action against Third World poverty and debt.

Within Britain, the Green Party's spectacular result in the 1989 European elections indicates that Green-Left co-operation around similar policies is also of growing relevance to the success of progressive politics at Westminster. Our most urgent task is to establish a radical consensus rather than a centralist one, which will oust the Conservatives and set Britain on a course of environmental renewal and social renaissance.

However, despite the Greens vastly improved electoral performance and opinion poll ratings compared with the period prior to the 1989 European elections, it is still obvious that under the present unjust electoral system they have little chance of winning any seats in Parliament, let alone being able to form a government to put their policies into practice.

Likewise, though Labour's poll results took a dramatic upward turn in mid–1989, it is still far from clear that Labour can win an outright majority at the next election. It would take an unprecedented electoral swing. In earlier parliaments since 1979, Labour's mid-term lead in the opinion polls was subsequently dramatically reversed and resulted in the massive defeats of 1983 and 1987.

Rather than risk a fourth Tory victory, it would seem sensible for the Greens and Labour to put aside any inclination to political vanity and electoral egoism which could well sustain the Conservatives in office. Instead, if we are genuinely concerned about preventing ecological catastrophe and overcoming social inequalities, Labour and the Greens should be willing to forego their differences and come to an electoral agreement involving a single Labour or Green candidate to defeat the Tories in one hundred target constituencies. The key basis for this agreement would be a commitment to introduce electoral reform and to call a second election, under a PR system, within two years. Given that it might take this long to get such legislation through parliament, there might also need to be agreed commitments on interim policies for environmental protection and social justice.

For Greens, a pact with Labour clearly makes more sense than the alternative proposal of a Green-Democrat electoral arrangement. Despite their green rhetoric, the Democrats are committed to a profit-oriented, free market economy with its intrinsically competitive and acquisitive impulses and geared towards ever greater economic expansion and capital accumulation for the benefit of a privileged minority. This type of economy is anathema to the Green vision of a co-operative and human need-centred society geared to the common good and ecological sustainability (a vision which tends to accord very closely with basic socialist values).

Furthermore, given the now marginal public support for the Democrats, the combined Green and Democrat vote could never add up to an electoral majority for government and would probably not even be sufficient to result in the election of a single Green MP. If the Greens are serious about winning political power to put their ideas into practice, then a pact with the Democrats is a non-starter. It is a recipe for continued powerlessness and marginalization.

In contrast, given that Labour's substantial body of public support *does* give it the potential to win an election and form a government, Green and Socialist collaboration makes much more sense.

This is not to deny the ecological deficiencies of some aspects of official Labour policy such as the fudge over nuclear power. However, Greens need to decide whether they are interested in political purity (is there such a thing as a pure political party?) or in practical action around the many other commitments that Labour shares in common with them: opposition to the poll tax and water privatization, defence of the National Health Service and local government, support for public transport and energy conservation, and agreement on the need to create Ministries for Women and Environmental Protection.

Though there are still too many Labour Party members wedded to state socialism and industrial productivism, Labour is definitely moving in a green direction and there has always been a commitment among much of the grassroots membership to a GLC-style socialism based on radical decentralization, popular participation, and sustainable economics. Surely, whatever their understandable misgivings about aspects of Labour policy, Greens ought to be linking up with these ecologically-aware socialists to strengthen their position within the Labour Party and to help pressure the leadership into a stronger green commitment.

Ultimately, the case for Green and Socialist solidarity rests on the recognition that our planet faces ecological disaster and that progressive political alliances which can help prevent such catastrophe merit support.

Indeed, if the ecological crisis is a genuine threat to human survival, then a Green-Labour electoral pact to win power and enact environment-saving legislation is a moral imperative. Moreover, such a pact would have a very desirable ecologically radicalizing influence on Labour consciousness and policies.

Naturally, an election agreement between Greens and Socialists needs to be democratically agreed by both parties at leadership and grassroots level in order to work. In a party system unused to collaboration, this is obviously a longer-term project and would require the creation of a new political culture which puts a premium on co-operation and solidarity between all progressive movements. This would involve our acceptance of the everyday facts of political life experienced by most of the Green and Socialist parties in the rest of Europe where alliances, pacts and coalitions are an integral part of the radical political agenda.

So far as the specifics of a Labour-Green electoral arrangement are concerned, it would focus on the fifty parliamentary seats in the six Euro-constituencies where the Greens came second to the Tories in 1989, and on a comparable number of Tory-Labour marginals elsewhere. In the former case, Labour would stand down to back the Green candidate. In the latter case, the Greens would withdraw to support Labour. Even if the transfer of votes from Labour to Green, and vice versa, was only successful in winning a third of these one hundred seats, this electoral pact could still make the difference between Tory victory and defeat in a tight poll and it would almost certainly give the Greens their first ever representatives at Westminster.

On the assumption that Labour may fall short of an overall majority in the House of Commons at the next election, a pact which resulted in the return of Green MPs could enable Labour to form a minority government with informal Green support. Alternatively, Labour could form an official Red-Green coalition, with the Greens becoming junior partners in government (as has already happened in the West German cities of Berlin and Frankfurt).

In circumstances where Labour was able to maintain at least a small lead over the Tories in the run-up to the next election, a Green-Labour pact would probably give Labour a substantial majority in parliament in its own right and a clear mandate to enact emergency measures for environmental security and social welfare pending the passage of PR legislation and the calling of a second election under a new electoral system.

The likely success of this strategy of electoral agreements would be further enhanced if similar deals could be struck with the Scottish National Party and Plaid Cymru (both of which have strong Green and Socialist currents within them) to make Scotland and Wales Tory-free zones.

Critics of this approach to ousting the Conservatives offer four major objections:

First, Ken Livingstone and others have argued that electoral pacts are unnecessary if we have PR because it would end the situation where the Tories get a majority of seats on a minority of votes.

Quite so. But we haven't yet got PR and the next election will be fought on the present disproportional system. We therefore need to devise a way of defeating the Tories under the existing electoral rules. Despite all the difficulties, some kind of election agreement (including agreement at constituency level) seems the most plausible way of achieving this. Indeed, it's notable that apart from the faith-like hope of an outright Labour victory, the opponents of this approach have singularly failed to offer any credible alternative strategy to get rid of the Tories.

A second and more substantial objection is that under the leadership of Neil Kinnock there is no way the Labour Party will ever agree to an electoral deal or to proportional representation.

For the immediate future, this is probably true. However, there is already a big and growing groundswell of support for electoral reform within Labour's grassroots membership, as indicated by the large number of resolutions on the subject at the 1989 party conference. Though defeated, the surge of these resolutions clearly indicates the way the tide is running within the Labour Movement. When it comes to the run-up to the next election, if Labour's fortunes slide (as occurred in 1983 and 1987), and if the party looks unable to defeat the Tories on its own, then the demands from within Labour's ranks for pacts and PR are likely to snowball, even among the leadership.

After more than a decade out of office, the one thing Labour's leaders desperately want is power. In recent years, they have repeatedly shown their willingness to dump old policies in favour of more electorally expedient ones. If they are prepared to compromise on key issues like defence for the sake of political power, there is a high probability that the party leadership would also be open to compromise on the questions of electoral agreements and PR, especially if they thought there were votes in it. A MORI poll in September 1989 showed that 3 per cent of non-Labour voters would switch to Labour if it supported PR. In a close-run election, this could be the margin between winning and losing. The Labour hierarchy is aware of this and therefore a sudden conversion to PR in the run-up to a tight poll is quite possible.

As for what needs to be done here and now, instead of bemoaning the Labour Party's present backwardness on electoral reform, supporters of PR from all parties ought to be doing everything in their power to help those of us on the inside who are trying to change the party's policy. Winning the Labour Party to PR is the key to implementing electoral reform. The Tories will never introduce PR because it would probably permanently exclude them from office. Under the present voting system, none of the anti-Tory parties, apart from Labour, has sufficient electoral support to win a majority of seats, form a government and legislate for PR. Labour's policy on electoral reform is therefore decisive and there can be no move to PR in the foreseeable future without first winning Labour's backing for it.

A third objection is that an electoral arrangement between Labour and the Greens, and the subsequent introduction of PR, would result in a hung parliament with Labour winning the most seats but not an overall majority. This would mean Labour forming a minority government with Green support. Such a scenario, it is argued, would end up with a political fudge and a betrayal of both Green and Socialist principles.

Not necessarily. From a Left perspective, being a minority government would have a radicalizing influence on Labour, forcing it to take on board the important unilateralist, ecological and decentralist demands of the Greens in order to win their support and stay in office; while from a Green point of view, co-operation with Labour would give them PR, their first group of MPs and begin the process of putting Green policies into practice and moving our society towards a more sustainable and humanitarian future. However imperfect, this has to be preferable to the present denial of parliamentary representation to the 2.3 million people who voted Green in the 1989 European elections and to the current ruination of our society by an ecologically exterministic economy.

A fourth objection to a Red-Green political alliance is that many Greens feel that Labour is just too tainted and compromised for them to contemplate co-operation. This is an understandable feeling given Labour's often appalling record in government. But is there any guarantee that Greens would not make similar compromises if they had to deal with the realities of power? Looking at what elected Green representatives are already doing in some West German cities where they are in coalition with the Social Democrats, I doubt it.

Perhaps it's time we faced up to the truth that there is no perfect political party. Every party has its flaws, including Labour and the Greens. There are strengths and weaknesses on both sides.

The Green Party, for example, despite its laudable commitment to ecological sustainability, has completely failed to specify the concrete policies required for the ecological conversion of the economy. Equally alarming, just when some of us on the Left are trying to take to heart the Greens' call for a new way of doing politics, a section of the Green Party is rapidly collapsing into the arrogance, manoeuvring and sectarianism of the traditional parties which they have previously so rightly condemned. These attitudes, which also exist among many on the Left, need to be challenged if we are to achieve the kind of pluralistic, broad-based, popular and radical realignment of progressive politics which is necessary to defeat the Conservatives.

Far from being a sell-out of Green or Socialist principles, electoral solidarity between Labour and the Greens would be an important first step towards giving radicals from both parties the much needed and long delayed parliamentary power to begin the ecological and egalitarian transformation of British society.

# References


## Introduction

1. Goldsmith, E., *et al, Blueprint for Survival*, Harmondsworth, Penguin, 1972.
2. *The Guardian*, March 27, 1989.
3. For a recent report on environmental damage see The World Commission on Environment and Development, *Our Common Future*, Oxford University Press, 1987.
4. There are many good books on Gramsci including Boggs, C., *Gramsci's Marxism*, London, Pluto, 1977; Fermia, J. V., *Gramsci's Political Thought*, Oxford University Press, 1981; and Showstack Sasson, A., *Gramsci's Politics*, London, Croom Helm, 1980. It is also worth looking at what Gramsci had to say; Gramsci, A., *Selections from Prison Notebooks*, Lawrence and Wishart, London, 1971 is very useful for this.

## 1: Another green world?

1. Williams, R., 'Beyond Actually Existing Socialism', in *Problems in Materialism and Culture*, London, Verso, 1980, p. 261.
2. Callenbach, E., *Ecotopia*, London, Pluto, 1978.
3. Wilde, O., 'The Soul of Man under Socialism', in *De Profundis and Other Writings*, Harmondsworth, Penguin, 1987, p. 34.
4. Goldsmith, E., *et al., Blueprint for Survival*, Harmondsworth, Penguin, 1972.
5. Ehrenfeld, D., 'Three million cheers for diversity', *New Scientist*, 12th June, 1986, pp. 38–43.
6. Cockburn, A., 'Trees, Cows and Cocaine: an Interview with Susanna Hecht', *New Left Review* No. 173, January/February 1989, pp. 34–55.
7. The World Commission on Environment and Development, *Our Common Future*, Oxford University Press, 1987, p. 149.
8. See ref. 5.
9. See ref. 5.
10. International Institute for Environment and Development, *World Resources*, New York, Basic, 1987, pp. 134–5.
11. *op. cit.*

12. 'Tropical Forests: A plan for action', *The Ecologist*, Vol. 17, No. 4/5, 1987, p. 129.
13. Mackenzie, D., 'An uphill battle to save Filipino trees', *New Scientist*, 30th June 1988, pp. 42–3.
14. 'Tropical Forests: A plan for action', *The Ecologist*, Vol. 17, No. 4/5, 1987, p. 129.
15. *op cit.*
16. Caulfield, C., 'Amazon rainforest project hurtles towards disaster', *New Scientist*, 26th February 1987, p. 24.
17. 'The restless deserts continue to grow', *New Scientist*, 26th February 1987, p. 26.
18. George, S., *How the Other Half Dies*, Harmondsworth, Penguin, 1976.
19. Rackham, O., *The History of the Countryside*, London, Dent, 1986.
20. Clarke, D., *Mesolithic Europe: the Economic Base*, London, Duckworth.
21. *The Independent*, 8th July, 1989.
22. Lovelock, J. E., *Gaia: A new look at life on Earth*, Oxford University Press, 1979.
23. Lean, G., 'The Big Heat', *The Observer*, 3rd July 1988.
24. Pearce, F., 'Ozone threat spreads from the Arctic', *New Scientist*, 24th March 1988, pp. 22–5.
25. 'Green Politics – The Facts', *New Internationalist*, No. 171, May 1987, pp. 16–17.
26. Bertell, R., *No Immediate Danger*, London, Women's Press, 1985.
27. See ref. 6.
28. The World Commission on Environment and Development, *Our Common Future*, Oxford University Press, 1987, pp. 32–3.
29. See ref. 5.
30. Pimental, S. and D., in Dahlberg, K., *et al*, *New Directions for Agriculture and Agricultural Research: Neglected Dimensions and Emerging Alternatives*, New Jersey, Rowman and Allenheld, 1986, p. 278.
31. Trainer, F. E., *Developed to Death*, London, Green Print, 1989.
32. Kapuśkiński, R., *The Emperor*, London, Picador, 1984, p. 140.
33. *op cit.* p. 64.
34. Wachtel, H. M., *The Politics of International Money*, Amsterdam, Transnational Institute, 1987.
35. Green, F., and Sutcliffe, B., *The Profit System*, London, Penguin, 1987, p. 332.
36. *op cit.* p. 334.
37. *Manifesto for a Sustainable Society*, London, The Green Party, 1988.
38. Thoreau, H. D., *Walden*, London, Dent, 1910, p. 5.
39. See ref. 34.
40. *New Internationalist*, No. 171, May 1987, p. 22.
41. Tatchell, P., *Democratic Defence*, London, Heretic, 1985.
42. Mellor, M., 'An Economy Fit for Women To live in?', *New Ground* No. 22, 1989, pp. 8–9.
43. Cockburn, C., *Machinery of Dominance*, London, Pluto, 1985, p. 7.
44. Huxley, A., *The Island*, London, Chatto and Windus, 1962, pp. 211–2.

## 2: *Unfortunate solutions*


1. Lean, G., 'The Big Heat?', *The Observer*, 3rd July 1988.
2. Goldsmith, E., *et al*, *Blueprint for Survival*, Harmondsworth, Penguin, 1972.
3. Meadows, D. H., and D. L., Randers, J., Behrens, W. W., III, *The Limits to Growth*, New York, Universe, 1972.
4. *The Global Report 2000 for the President*, Harmondsworth, Penguin, 1982.
5. *op cit.*, p. 1.
6. The World Commission on Environment and Development, *Our Common Future*, Oxford University Press, 1987.
7. CDU party worker to author, Baden-Baden, West Germany, January 1987.
8. Komarov, B., *The Destruction of Nature in the Soviet Union*, London, Pluto, 1978.
9. *op cit.*
10. Beckerman, W., *Pricing for Pollution*, Institute of Economic Affairs, 1975.
11. Elkington, J., *The Green Capitalists: Industry's search for Environment Excellence*, London, Gollancz, 1987.
12. See ref. 10.
13. Lovelock, J. E., *Gaia: A new look at life on Earth*, Oxford University Press, 1979.
14. Mackenzie, D., 'An uphill battle to save Filipino trees', *New Scientist*, 30th June, 1988, pp. 42–43.
15. See ref. 13.
16. *Green Anarchist* proclaims 'GOAL: Autonomous self-sufficient villages, bringing regression of technology; no industry, no bomb, no pollution, no hunger, no bomb.'
17. Ehrenfeld, D., *The Arrogance of Humanism*, Oxford University Press, 1978.
18. Lovelock, J. E., *Gaia: A new look at life on Earth*, Oxford University Press, 1979.
19. Hardin, G. and Baden, J., *Managing the Commons*, San Franciso, W. H. Freeman, 1977, p. 263.
20. Bookchin, M., *Green Perspectives*, Burlington, Green Program Project, 1988.
21. Goldsmith, E., *The Great U-Turn*, Bideford, Green Books, 1988, p. 17.
22. Heilbronner, R. L., *An Inquiry into the Human Prospect*, New York, Norton, 1974.
23. See ref. 19, p. 26.
24. Nicholson, M., *The Environmental Revolution*, Harmondsworth, Penguin, 1972.
25. Ashby, Sir E., letter in *The Ecologist*, Vol. 2, No. 4, 1972, p. 23.
26. Goldsmith, E., *The Great U-Turn*, Bideford, Green Books, 1988. See Chapter One, The Fall of the Roman Empire.
27. Macfarlane, L. J., letter in *The Ecologist*, Vol. 3, No. 1, 1973, p. 39.
28. Dumont, R., 'Manifesto of an Alternative Culture', *Undercurrents*, No. 10, March-April 1975, p. 18.
29. Saville, J., *The Labour Movement in Britain*, London, Faber and Faber, 1988.

30. Mullin, C., *A Very British Coup*. Corgi, London, 1988.
31. Molyneux, J., 'Marxism in the Greenhouse', *Socialist Worker*, 16 July 1988, p. 9.
32. *op cit.*

## *3:Structure*

1. Network for Alternative Technology and Technology Assessment, *Alternative Technology: An Answer to the Energy Crisis*, Milton Keynes, NATTA, 1980, p. 7.
2. Priest, C., *A Dream of Wessex*, London, Pan, 1977.
3. Trainer, F. E., *Abandon Affluence!* London, Zed, 1985, p. 250.
4. The statistics in this section are from *New Internationalist*, May 1989, No. 195, p. 16–17.
5. Parkin, S., *Green Parties: An International Guide*, London, Heretic, 1989.
6. See ref. 4.
7. Smith, I., 'Making Money out of a City's Waste Mountain', *Sunday Times*, 9th July, 1989, p. F3.
8. Burnett, B., 'Green Guardians', *The Vegan*, Vol. 4, No. 2, Summer 1980, pp. 8–9.
9. Gradwohl, J. and Greenberg, R., *Saving the Tropical Forests*, London, Earthscan, 1988, pp. 122–5.
10. For a description of the chinampas before and after the arrival of the Conquistadores see Redclift, M., 'Redefining the Environmental "Crisis" in the South', in Weston, J. (Ed.), *Red and Green*, London, Pluto, 1986, pp. 82–86.
11. Bahro, R., *Building the Green Movement*, Heretic, London, 1986, p. 12.
12. Reece, R., *The Sun Betrayed*, Boston, South End Press, 1979, p. 211.
13. John, R., Review of *The Sun Betrayed*, *Telos*, No. 48, 1981, p. 237.
14. Schwartz Cohen, R., 'How the Refrigerator Got Its Hum', in Mackenzie, D. and Wajeman, J., *The Social Shaping of Technology*, Milton Keynes, Open University Press, 1985, pp. 202–218.
15. *op cit.* p. 214.
16. Bramwell, A., *Ecology in the 20th Century*, New Haven, Yale University Press, 1989, p. 89.
17. *The Guardian*, 17th March, 1989.
18. Nicholls, P. (ed.), *The Encyclopedia of Science Fiction*, London, Granada, 1981, p. 376.
19. Cooley, M., 'Drawing up the Corporate Plan at Lucas Aerospace', in Mackenzie, D. and Wajeman, J., *The Social Shaping of Technology*, Milton Keynes, Open University Press, 1985, pp. 165–172.
20. White Jr., L., *Medieval Religion and Social Change*, University of California Press, 1978, pp. 270–1.

## *4:Politics*

1. Lewis, N., and Bleyer, P., 'Die Grünen in conference', *Interlink*, No. 8, August-September, 1988, p. 17.
2. Brown, P. and Milne, R., 'Seal studies stumble through lack of money', *New Scientist* 1st September, 1989, p. 29.

3. *The Vegan*, Summer 1989, p. 7.
4. Carver, J., 'Comrades or Clients', *New Ground*, No. 3, 1984, pp. 9–10.
5. Bray, J., *The Politics of the Environment*, Fabian Tract No. 412, London, Fabian Society.
6. Sullivan, A. W., *Greening the Tories*, London, Centre for Policy Studies, 1985, p. 41.
7. Parkin, S., *Green Parties: An International Guide*, London, Heretic, 1989.
8. Parkin, S., 'The Battle for Brazil', *Econews*, No. 45, July 1989, p. 3.
9. Inglehart, R., 'Post-Materialism in an Environment of Insecurity', *American Political Science Review*, Vol. 75, No. 4, 1981.
10. Rennard, C., *Winning Local Elections*, Hebden Bridge, West Yorkshire, Association of Liberal Councillors, 1988.
11. Using such a strategy we increased our vote in Walcot ward of Bath City Council from 5% in 1987, to 11% in 1988, 23.5% in late '88 in spite of it being a closely fought Conservative/Labour marginal.
12. Irvine, S., and Ponton, A., *A Green Manifesto*, London, Optima, 1988, p. 145.
13. Lipset, S. M., Introduction to Michels, R., *Political Parties*, New York, Free Press/Macmillan, 1968, p. 18.
14. Brian, M., *Changing the Cogs*, Canberra, Friends of the Earth, 1979, p. 81.
15. Pearce, F., 'Fear of the dole keeps Britain's dirtiest factory open'. *New Scientist*, 18th June 1981, p. 745.
16. This was said to be one of the factors that allowed the Conservative to retain Kensington during the July 1988 by-election.
17. *Edge of Darkness* was a BBC thriller that examined state power and the threat to 'Gaia' from nuclear power. It was first broadcast in 1987 causing a considerable stir.
18. Gandhi quoted in *Green Line*, Oxford, November, 1982, p. 31.
19. Marx, K., *Capital*, Vol. 1., Preface to the First Edition, Harmondsworth, Penguin, p. 92.

## *5:Economics*

1. Dauncey, G., *After the Crash*, London, Green Print, 1988.
2. It is interesting to note the sexism of both right and left categories here.
3. Nove, A., *The Economics of Feasible Socialism*, London, Allen and Unwin, 1983, p. 5.
4. *op cit.* p. 33.
5. Frankel, B., *The Post-Industrial Utopians*, Cambridge, Polity, 1987.
6. Trainer, F. E., *Abandon Affluence!*, London, Zed, 1985, p. 279.
7. Slater, P., *Wealth Addiction*, New York, E. P. Dutton, 1980, pp. 155–97.
8. Burns, T., 'The Revolution Betrayed', *Solidarity*, No. 16, Spring 1988.
9. Aguirre, C. and Klonsky, M., *As Soon as this Pub Closes . . .* , Bristol, Full Marks, 1988.
10. Elkington, J., *The Green Capitalists: Industry's search for Environment Excellence*, London, Gollancz, 1987.
11. Castells, M., *City, Class and Power*, London, Macmillan, 1978, p. 157.
12. Dauncey, G., *After the Crash*, London, Green Print, 1988, pp. 52–69.

13. Barratt Brown, M., *Models in the Political Economy*, Harmondsworth, Pelican, 1984, p. 256.
14. See ref. 5, pp. 55–63.
15. Slater, P., *Wealth Addiction*, New York, E. P. Dutton, 1980, p. 131.
16. Norton Taylor, R., *Whose Land is it Anyway?*, London, Turnstone, 1982.
17. Nove, A., *The Economics of Feasible Socialism*, London, George Allen and Unwin, 1983, pp. 46–7.
18. Illich, I., *Tools for Conviviality*, London, Fontana, 1975, p. 60.
19. Slater, P., *Wealth Addiction*, New York, E. P. Dutton, 1980, p. 131.
20. Fromm, E., *To Have or to Be*, London, Abacus, 1976.
21. Roberts, A., *The Self-Managing Society*, London, Allison and Busby, 1979, p. 33.
22. Schumacher, F. E., *Small is Beautiful*, London, Abacus, 1974, pp. 52–53.
23. Slater, P., *Wealth Addiction*, New York, E. P. Dutton, 1980, p. 4.

## *6:Belief*

1. Huxley, A., *Brave New World*, Grafton, London, 1987, p. 12.
2. Lukes, S., *Power: A Radical View*, London, Macmillan, 1974, p. 24.
3. White, L., Jr., 'The Historical Roots of our Ecologic Crisis', *Science*, 1967, no. 155, pp. 1203–1207.
4. Mumford, L., *The Myth of the Machine*, New York, Harcourt, Brace and Wood, 1966, p. 195.
5. Capra, F., *The Turning Point*, London, Flamingo, 1984, p. 25.
6. Marx, K., *The German Ideology*, reprinted in Thompson, J., and Tunstall, K., *Sociological Perspectives*, Harmondsworth, Penguin, 1971, p. 47.
7. Padadakis, E., *The Green Movement in West Germany*, Beckenham, Croom Helm, 1984.
8. Frankel, B., *The Post Industrial Utopians*, Cambridge, Polity, 1987.
9. *Crisis* is published every fortnight by Fleetway Publications, 3rd floor, Greater London House, Hampstead Road, London NW1.
10. Comment from Michael Bruchmann to the author.
11. Fromm, E., *To Have or to Be*, London, Abacus, 1976.

## *Journals*

*Change*. A magazine for Eco-socialism and beyond edited by Peter Tatchell, Jeremy Seabrook and others. Available from Spring 1990.
*Capitalism, Nature and Socialism*. The only international theoretical and political journal of socialist ecology is obtainable from P.O. Box 8467, Santa Cruz, California 95061, U.S.A., for $7.00 inclusive of postage and packing.

# Index

# Green Print

We are independent publishers of books on green and environmental issues. Our list is expanding rapidly, and is widely available through bookshops.

Most of our titles are published as paperbacks at very competitive prices. They cover a very wide range of interests.

To receive our catalogue and join our free mailing list, please write to Green Print, 10 Malden Road, London NW5 3HR.